England for a Change

ETHEL MANNIN

England
for a Change

THE TRAVEL BOOK CLUB
121 CHARING CROSS ROAD
LONDON WC2

HUTCHINSON & CO (Publishers) LTD
178–202 Great Portland Street, London W1

London Melbourne Sydney
Auckland Bombay Toronto
Johannesburg New York

First impression 1968
Second impression September 1968

Printed in Great Britain
by The Anchor Press Ltd,
Tiptree, Essex

To

CHERRY KEARTON

who years ago said,
'Why don't you write
about England, for
a change . . . ?'

Acknowledgements

For permission to use the photograph of the interior of the great hall of St. Mary's Hospital (almshouses), Chichester, I am indebted to the present Custos, the Reverend H. M. J. Burdett. The photograph of the new cathedral, Coventry, is reproduced from *Cathedral Reborn* by courtesy of English Counties Periodicals, Ltd., Leamington Spa, to whom I am also indebted for the photograph of the Virgin and Child in the Lady Chapel of the Cathedral of Christ the King, Liverpool, and the photograph of the exterior of the cathedral. For the photograph of 'Captain "Long John" Silver' I am indebted to his widow, Mrs. Lois Cumbers.

I gratefully acknowledge my indebtedness to Frank Carr, C.B., C.B.E., for his patient answering of questions in connection with Greenwich and the *Cutty Sark*; and for the loan of books, and much other valuable help, not least driving me to a number of places not easily accessible by train, I am deeply indebted to my old friend Gilbert Turner.

E.M.

Contents

I

Lavender Hill Revisited

'Go back to source,' urged my publisher, in the person of Mr. Gerald Austin, when we were sitting in a pub off Great Portland Street and discussing how best to plan this book. 'Go back to Clapham, revisit Lavender Hill which you wrote about in your *Confessions* in connection with your childhood. Begin with the part of England you sprang from, the south London where you were born . . .'

A sentimental pilgrimage back into the past, to the beginning of the century; and I was never a one for retracing steps.

'It'll all be different,' I pointed out. 'Re-developed, with super-markets and tall blocks.'

'All right,' he cried, enthusiastically. 'Report it! Relate your childhood memories of it all to the present day—to swinging London! Isn't that what the book's to be about—England today? The impact of the changing times? Let me get you another drink.'

I let him, and we went on talking and my initial resistance subsided: it began to seem an idea. I promised to make a trip 'up the junction' the following Saturday morning. Clapham Junction certainly was still there, and the big stores, Arding and Hobbs, across the road from it, and Clapham Common, and, I supposed, Lavender Hill itself, unless they'd changed the name of it: perhaps even Garfield Road, off it, where I was born, and where my brother was born, three years later.

In my childhood memories Clapham Junction was the exciting place we went to once a year, in the summer, driven there in a horse-cab, with our tin trunk beside the driver, to spend a holiday with grand-parents on a farm in Surrey. It was an event of major importance; the cab was ordered the day before, and on the day there were endless anxious peepings through the lace curtains of our upstairs windows—we had the upper half of the house in Garfield Road—to see if it had arrived. When it did we had the pride and satisfaction of other people peeping through their curtains to witness our splendid departure. We always arrived at the junction much too early and had a long wait sitting on the platform, beside the tin trunk, watching the steam trains thundering through on their way to the coast. They were called express trains and they did not stop until they reached their destinations; but the train that eventually came for us stopped, obligingly, everywhere, and for all its puffing and blowing and air of importance was not, truth to tell, going very far; but this I did not know, because anywhere away from home was very far.

Lavender Hill in memory was the place where Mother did her Saturday shopping, with baby brother in the pram, and a string bag dangling from the handles, and me stumbling along beside, frequently admonished not to 'scuffle', but pick my feet up, and to 'keep up with the pram'. In the light afternoons of spring and summer we must have shopped in daylight, but in memory it is always dark on Lavender Hill, with naptha flares on the costermongers' barrows at which the fruit and vegetables were bought. One memory there is of Lavender Hill in daylight, and that is shortly after my brother was born and my mother was still in bed—'to keep the new baby warm' —going with an aunt to buy the big white shawl to wrap him in.

Clapham Common was the wide open space of grass shiny

with the sun on it, and of gorse bushes—I am sure there are none there now—whose yellow flowers could be pulled off, avoiding the sharp prickles all round them, and put into a small basket. It was also the place where one day walking with my father we met a very important man. The man and my father talked together, and when we got home my father told my mother about it, in a pleased way. Years later I knew that the man was John Burns, the socialist member of parliament, whom my father admired very much; as boys they had sung together in the same choir in Westminster, where my father was born. But all this I have told elsewhere. [1]

All that was at the beginning of the century; now in the late 'sixties I was going back, making the first of my journeys for this book about England; in a sense the longest journey of all —the journey more than sixty years back into the past.

I crossed the busy cross-roads outside Clapham Junction over to the emporium of Arding and Hobbs, with its domes of rare device, and began the ascent of Lavender Hill. For a long time it seemed a shopping thoroughfare like any other, with shops selling television sets, washing-machines, glass and china, furniture; women's dress shops, and men's outfitters with the Carnaby Street touch; the standard food shops: shops neither elegant nor drab, but ordinary, just very lower middle-class ordinary. At the top of the hill a turning went off at a right-angle, Lavender Sweep. The hill descended and there was Lavender Walk, and Lavender Gardens. All was grey, common-place, nondescript. I trudged on through the cold grey March wind and began to be worried; did memory, then, play one completely false? Surely there had been a pavement with a step up to a higher level and Mother had propped the pram up against shop windows on that higher level, with the pavement descending in broad tiers to the maelstrom of the road, churning with its horse-drawn traffic of vans and cabs and

1. In *Confessions and Impressions*, 1929, and *This was a Man, some Memories of Robert Mannin*, 1952.

trams, interlaced with bicycles? And then, suddenly reassuring-
ly, it was there—the two-tiered pavement, the step up to the
shops, and at the corner three steps down to the road, and there
was Garfield Road, with its respectable-looking Victorian
houses—and, incredibly, there at the corner was the timber
yard which so excitingly caught fire one night, its flames
leaping to the skies and our upstairs windows becoming hot
and the fire-engines charging in with bells crashing on the
bridles of the horses and the fire gleaming on the brass helmets
of the firemen.

The traffic was still a maelstrom below the tiered pavement,
though there was not a horse in sight, but across the road an
awning came out across the stalls outside a greengrocer's shop
on a corner, *just as it always had*, and round the corner, and the
corner of the preceding turning, there were stalls piled high
with fruit and vegetables, with protective half-screens round,
flanked by bunches of flowers—daffodils and wallflowers. Of
course there were wallflowers; there always had been, we
always seemed to come home with a bunch of wallflowers at
the top of the string bag, or at the foot of the pram. A bunch of
wallflowers, and four ounces of sweets, which you got for a
penny; better-quality sweets were two ounces a penny, but the
four-ounces-a-penny were good enough for us. A farthing had
value in those days; it would buy you an ounce of sweets or a
sheet of pins—which were often given in lieu of a farthing
change at the draper's, when things cost one-and-eleven-three,
as they often did, and you tendered a florin.

This was Lavender Hill as I had remembered it, from 1903,
the stepped pavements, the awning out over the greengrocer's
on the corner, the street stalls, with the fruit and flowers and
vegetables, the timber yard at the corner of Garfield Road. That
end of the hill, where it dips down steeply, is quite different
from 'up the junction'. It loses its lower-middle-class gentility
here and takes on a rough virility instead, the good coarse
natural stuff of living. No damn nonsense down here. Take it

or leave it. There are a lot of coloured people about—every other person seems to be a West Indian. For the most part they are young, attractive, well-dressed. Some of the young men look like students, and they all have an air of being completely at home in this grey south London environment. With their dark skins they nevertheless bring colour to the scene, and a kind of vitality. There are pregnant young women, small children, babies in prams. There are bright clothes, and wonderful teeth flashing in rich black laughter.

The road goes plunging on through a grey congested density to Stockwell and the city, to which my father as a young man journeyed every day, by horse-tram or by bicycle, to the General Post Office, Mount Pleasant, to sort letters in the Inland Section, six and sometimes seven days a week, and this he did for forty years.

I turn up into Garfield Road and walk along the left-hand side, and a little way up, not quite half way, I stop, for I think that this is the house where my brother and I were born, near enough to the timber yard on the other side to feel the heat from the fire on our windows, but not so near that we were in any danger. Whilst I stand looking at the house, looking up to the rooms we inhabited, the front door opens and a young black woman comes out and takes in some bottles of milk; small children crowd behind her. I walk on and a young black man is doing something to a car; on the other side of the road two young black girls walk talking and laughing together, and a black man comes out of a house. They are all neat and respectable-looking, and the houses appear well-kept, with neat curtains—'You can always tell by the curtains,' my mother used to say, when assessing the respectability or otherwise of the other people in the various roads in which we lived, in Tooting and South Wimbledon, when we left Clapham.

Now something curious happened to me there in Garfield Road, for I had no idea at all as to the relation of Clapham Common with Lavender Hill, but I wanted very much to come to it, retracing my steps back into the remote past, and for some reason I did not want to ask anyone, because all the people about me, both black and white, belonged to the present, and I walked amongst them as a kind of ghost from the past. I walked on, with no sense of direction, and followed the road round its L-shaped bend. Somewhere within myself, buried under a deep rubble of the years, was knowledge of a wall; a high wall, along which my mother, pushing the pram, with me at her side, scuffling and not keeping up, made her way to the Common. What happened to me was the re-assertion of this forgotten knowledge; I walked blindly, with no concious knowing, but also I walked instinctively, guided by this subconscious memory.

I followed the road round and came to a new housing estate of council houses, and this had nothing to do with me, it was something outside my terms of reference; there were bungalows in the foreground and blocks of flats, not high, behind; it was a pleasant-looking estate, but it had nothing to do with me; I was looking for a wall. There had to be a wall or the whole world of memory was lost. And then beyond the estate I came to it, high, with dark old brick, and budding lilacs, and almond blossom, and with forsythia in triumphant yellow flower crowding over. Half of it, I then realised, had been knocked down when the housing estate had been created on the big garden it had enclosed. There had been a kind of alleyway, I now remembered, where the first part of the wall ended and the second part, enclosing another huge garden, began. The housing estate had done away with the alleyway, but the wall which had formed one side of it was still there, though now a modern garage was up against it.

I felt curiously happy walking along under the wall, because yet again memory had not played me false, because something more remained from the past, and because now I knew myself to be on the way to the Common, going the way we had always gone, along Wix Lane, and very clearly I saw my mother as she was then, young, dark-eyed, dark-haired, lively, walking jauntily, heading for the green open space of the Common, the new baby in the pram, the toddler scuffling along beside her or running on ahead. Everything was in order; we should come to an enormous house with a tower-like roof, and a conservatory on the first floor, at the side. We, not I, for the elderly woman marching alone on that grey March morning in 1967 was only the appearance of reality; the reality was March 1904, and my brother was two months old, I was nearly three and a half, and my mother was twenty-five. There was broken glass along the top of the wall; it was to stop people climbing over, my mother said, and it never occurred to me to ask how people could climb over so high a wall.

The huge old Victorian mansion, five storeys with a high steep roof surmounted with iron work, and decorations in stone work—vine-like leaves—round the deep arched win-dows, is still there, but the conservatory which so fascinated me as a child has been removed, leaving a discoloration on the wall to mark, plainly, where it had been. The window which formed a door opening out into it now opens on to the brick-walled verandah that once contained it. The house is called Cedar House, and there is an old cedar tree in the stretch of garden in front of it. It is the end house of a terrace; there is an identical terrace across the road from it, and the road is called Cedars Road. These terraces were built on the site of a house called The Cedars, so-called from the cedars in the grounds. According to J. H. Michael Burgess, in his *The Chronicles of Clapham*,[1] the house was pulled down in 1864 to clear the way for Cedars Road and these two terraces, but Dr. N. Pevsner, no less an authority on London, gives their date as 1860. He regards their creation as typical Mid-Victorian self-assertive-ness, and declares that they are of 'considerable importance for their date, 1860. The French pavilion roofs are amongst the first signs of that French Renaissance revival in London which

1. 1929.

culminates in such buildings as the Grosvenor Hotel, also by Knowles.' James Knowles designed the terraces, and St. Augustine's Church in Cedars Road. Pevsner continues harshly, 'The details are robust and tasteless; note especially the barbarous, wholly un-French, roundheaded window surrounds with their segment-headed windows and the space between the segment and the round top filled by gross foliage.'

'Gross foliage'—all those lovely vine-leaves! Whatever would Dr. Pevsner have made of the conservatory planked on the side of the first floor? All those lovely potted palms and aspidistras. My mother used to say that the conservatory was used by the ladies and gentlemen who came to the big house when there was a ball, and the room out of which the conservatory opened was all lit up by the glass things which hung from the ceiling and were called chandeliers.

But that is more than half a century ago, and the conservatory is no more, and the great house is now the University of Surrey, North Side Hall, and across the road from it is Clapham Common, North Side. Perhaps by the time this appears in print this Mid-Victorian mansion will no longer be there, for I am told that the University of Surrey is moving out to Guildford, which may mean that the site is scheduled for re-development, and a high building, all glass and concrete, will go up there; such buildings, I observed, already flank the West Side of the Common. Perhaps they are better in their lightness and brightness than the dark old Victoriana; certainly they better meet the needs of the times, and architecturally and aesthetically there is nothing to be said for buildings such as Cedar House, and we should not, I suppose, mourn the passing of something which has outlived its day and has no historic or aesthetic claims upon us.

Yet I stood a long time that March morning leaning against the wall of the house opposite, at the end of Wix Lane, looking at the dark pretentious ugliness of Cedar House, and the scar on the wall where the conservatory had been, endowing the house with such magic for a child. It seemed to me as I stood there that there was the same green-grass smell blowing off the Common that there had always been, though now motor traffic, with all its fumes, surged past on the main road.

I retraced my steps down Wix Lane and back into Garfield Road, and along the length of Garfield Road to Lavender Hill, where I crossed the road for the pleasure of going down the steps, and I looked at the street stalls and was pleased that there were bunches of wallflowers, and came to a shop which had a great deal of merchandise outside on the pavement— crockery, and pots and pans, and packets of detergent, all manner of household things, and all, according to the price cards, at knock-down prices. There were some non-stick frying pans at nine shillings, reduced from twenty-five ... well, perhaps. Anyhow, they were cheap at the price and I went in and bought one, then clutching my frying-pan continued on up Lavender Hill, noting an Asian Spice and Food Stores, and two African names on a doctors' brass plate in a terrace of black-brick Victorian houses. Side turnings descended steeply, flanked by drab terraced houses, to the railway line and a density of bricks and mortar, ugly, treeless, brutal. But it was all right; there was almond blossom and forsythia crowding over the wall in Wix Lane, and a green-grass smell blowing off the Common.

Vaguely, as I marched along with my frying-pan, I was look-ing for the church in which baby-brother had been christened; I remembered it as having a garden, with grass and shrubs, where for some reason, I had had to wait with an aunt, or someone, during the ceremony. I came to a massive brown hump of a church, more like a castle than a church, with candle-snuffer towers; it had a little garden with grass and shrubs, but it wasn't the church I was looking for, because it was Roman Catholic, and we were brought up very strictly C. of E., Sunday school and all. This church so much affronted me, both by its massive ugliness and by the disappointment it represented, that I crossed the road, offendedly, and it must have been my guardian angel who led me across for I found myself at the end of a long straight road called Lavender Gardens, with a church at the end of it, pleasantly ornate, with a pinnacled tower, very graceful.

I had no idea whether this was the church I was looking for, but I had a compulsion to go and look at it. On the way I passed a house which bore a plaque saying that G. A. Henty had lived there, 1832–1902. Those are the dates of his birth and death; I wondered when and for how long he had lived in Lavender Gardens. His boys' adventure stories were part of my childhood.

At the end of the road I came to the Common again, the North Side, and St. Barnabas Church, and it was quite certainly the church I was looking for, little grassy garden and all. The architectural style, I learned later, is 'Bassett Smith's usual flowing Decorated'. It was somehow important that I should have found the church; it rounded off my memories. Of the large, pale yellow, and floridly handsome Parochial Building next to the church I had no memory at all.

I retraced my steps down the very respectable Lavender Gardens, where there was nobody about, no sign of life at all, not even a cat sitting on a gate-post, to the Saturday morning crowds of Lavender Hill, all prams and children and shopping baskets and black people, the *hoi-polloi*. I re-crossed the road, because all the street stalls were on the other side, and there was one thing more I had to do before I went on 'up the junction'— buy a bunch of wallflowers . . .

2

Maritime Greenwich

WHEN I was in my favourite place in America, San Francisco, standing on the waterfront at Fisherman's Wharf and looking across to the fine old windjammer, the *Balclutha*, berthed there now as a national museum, I was suddenly homesick for my favourite place in London—perhaps in all England—Greenwich, and the lovely little clipper ship that dominates it, the *Cutty Sark*. The American ship is the last of the Cape Horners and some twenty years later than the *Cutty Sark*; she is a heavier ship, a 'deep-water man', with a steel hull; when she was built and launched in Glasgow in 1886 it was already late in the day for sailing ships; in her time—she was built in 1869—the *Cutty Sark* competed with the *Thermopylae* to be 'the fastest clipper afloat', but nearing the end of the nineteenth century the demand was for increased cargo capacity, and with bigger ships the speed and grace which characterised the *Cutty Sark* had to be sacrificed.

She was a fine old ship, the *Balclutha*, I thought, beautiful as all sailing ships are, and it was fine down there on Fisherman's Wharf, in the Californian sunshine and with the blue waters of the bay in front and the white skyscrapers of the city climbing up on the hills behind . . . but born-and-bred Londoner that I am I was homesick for London's murky old river, and the grey skies banked with cloud, and the noble twin domes and the pillared façades of Wren's buildings along the waterfront of Greenwich on the Thames—*maritime* Greenwich.

It is the title of an excellent little book, *Maritime Greenwich*,[1] written by Mr. Frank Carr, who was Director of the National Maritime Museum from 1947 until he retired in 1966, and I like it as a description of Greenwich because a principal joy of this Thames-side town is the feeling of its nearness to the sea, with cargo ships from Scandinavian countries, and from Holland, Belgium, and all over, coming up into the Pool of London, or with deep, mournful cries hurrying back down the river to the sea.

Greenwich lies five miles below Tower Bridge, on the Surrey side, and when the river passes Stepney on the other side, and the Lower Pool becomes Limehouse Beach, it sweeps round the peninsula of the Isle of Dogs in a great S bend on its way to Woolwich. Greenwich looks across to Millwall and riverside public gardens on the Isle of Dogs, so-called, some say, with *double entendre*, because King Charles II kept his bitches there. Though others, frowning upon such slander, say that he did in fact keep his dogs there when he lived at Greenwich Palace, though why he should live at one side of the river and keep his dogs on the other side is not explained. Another and more likely suggestion, is that the Isle of Dogs is a corruption of the Isle of Ducks—certainly in that great area of marshland there must have been many wildfowl. There is also the legend that a waterman murdered a man who had his dog with him, and that the dog swam to and fro across the river until the body of his master was found, and later snarled at a strange waterman who confessed, when accused of the murder, and was duly hanged. H. M. Tomlinson, who had a great love for London's river, and knew it well, offers no explanation in his book, *Below London Bridge*,[2] as to how the Isle of Dogs got its name, though he mentions it several times. But of the

1. Pitkin Pride of Britain Books, 1966.
2. 1934.

Greenwich waterfront he says that it is 'the most comely on the river'.

Many people when they make the trip by steamer from Westminster Bridge down to Greenwich make the mistake of going no further than the pier when they step ashore. To be sure, it is a very pleasant pier, gay in the summer with tubs and urns filled with geraniums and petunias, and with white-painted benches on which to sit and watch the river scene, and hot and cold drinks may be bought there and consumed under cover at an open-air place set out with chairs and tables, and many people just sit there and take light refreshments and look at the river and take the next steamer back; others do not even leave the steamer on which they arrived. Yet behind the pier, at the end of a short street, rises the lovely green hill of Greenwich Park, crowned by the buildings of the old Royal Observatory, now housing the most important astronomical collection in the world, and Flamsteed House, designed by Wren at the order of Charles II 'for the Observator's habitation and a little for pompe', and whose courtyard is crossed by the meridian line. And beside the pier there is the lovely ship, the *Cutty Sark*, her masts rising above the trees of the waterfront, and her presence dominating the town. The wonderful and famous view of Greenwich, as painted by Canaletto in the mid-eighteenth century and unchanged, today—'the most unaltered view in London', Frank Carr calls it—the Wren buildings of the old Royal Hospital for Seamen, now the Royal Naval College, is to be seen from the river as the steamer approaches, and a fine and stirring view it is, but it demands closer inspection, for great architectural and historical riches lie behind.

There is so much to delight and interest in Greenwich that in setting out to give an idea of it to anyone who has never been there it is difficult to know where to begin. I suppose the best introduction to Greenwich is to arrive by water, as I did myself the first time—and many times since—and then, after

the first exciting close-up of the *Cutty Sark*, leaving the tour of
the ship until later, resolutely to turn one's back on her and walk
along the waterfront to the old Trafalgar Tavern, which stands
with its feet in the water looking across to Millwall. It is a very
beautiful early nineteenth-century building, with its deep
windows under fan-shaped lead hoods, and it must have been
wonderful to have had a flat there when it ceased to be a
tavern; but recently it has been renovated and refurbished and
is now an elegant and expensive restaurant, with smart bars.
Down the passage way round the corner from it there is a
public-house called the Yacht which better suits both the purse
and the temperament of such as myself; there is a terrace at the
back overlooking the river, and on a summer noon or a
summer evening there is no pleasanter spot at which to sit and
drink and watch the ships hurrying down to the sea some
five-and-thirty miles away.

On the narrow promenade along to the Trafalgar Tavern
there is a fine view between the two wings of the Royal Naval
College of the white Palladian-style beauty of the Queen's
House lying back across the noble spaciousness of the Grand
Square and flanked by its long colonnades. It is venerated by
Americans as the inspiration for the White House. In the
summer the glow of massed red geraniums all along the base of
the colonnades makes it all like some brilliant stage-set. In
front of the Queen's House, on the park side, there is a wide
herbaceous border, like that at Hampton Court, and from the
top of the grassy hill of the park the house is seen to be set
exactly between the two wings of the Naval College, each with
its noble dome, at the other side of the Grand Square, and beyond, of course, completing the picture, flows the old grey
river.

From the top of the hill, too, is a fine view out over London
due north to the Hampstead heights, dimly outlined across the
smoky city with its tall chimneys and its foreground of cranes
and derricks rising from a labyrinth of docks and wharves and

quays. Usually a thin mist lies over London, but on a clear day the dome of St. Paul's Cathedral is to be seen between the twin towers of Tower Bridge. There are old hawthorn trees with twisted trunks on the hillside, and on a summer's day it is pleasant to lie on the grass in the shade of a tree and look out across the river to the City of London glistening through its greyness. Or, for the more sedate, there are benches at the top of the hill, in front of the statue of General Wolfe, perched on his pedestal, with the dome of the old Observatory behind him, and Flamsteed House, where the twenty-four-hour clock is set into the boundary wall, across from him. Wolfe stands there because he spent all his home and school life from the age of thirteen in Greenwich. The monument is a gift from the people of Canada; it was designed by a Canadian sculptor, Tait Mackenzie, and was unveiled by the Marquis of Montcalm in June, 1930. To the west, bounded by the high red brick wall with which James I enclosed the park between 1609 and 1625, there is General Wolfe Road, and Macartney House, the home of James Wolfe's parents from 1751. At that time Wolfe recorded, 'My father has offered money for the prettiest house situated in England.'

After the battle of Quebec Wolfe's body was brought home to Greenwich, where he was buried in the parish church of St. Alfege, which is on Stockwell Street and is hardly to be missed on entering the town. It was named after Alfege, the archbishop of Canterbury, who was brought there by the Danes in 1012, after their raid on Canterbury, and murdered by them on that spot when he refused to pay the ransom money. The present church was built there in 1718, by Nicholas Hawksmoor, a pupil of Wren's. Hawksmoor was at the time clerk of works for Wren's scheme for the Royal Hospital, which was later to become the Royal Naval College. The church is handsome, in the stately eighteenth-century manner. It was badly damaged in World War II, but, in Frank Carr's words, 'superbly restored' by Sir Albert Richardson. The tower, with its four clock faces, was not built until 1730. The original church built on the site collapsed when its roof caved in, in 1710, but the tower was left standing and was retained for a few more years when the new church was built. Some of the shops along that stretch of road where the church stands are the ground floors of eighteenth-century houses which have seen better days.

On Crooms Hill, leading up steeply from Stockwell Street, there are some very beautiful and even older houses, dating from the seventeenth century. One of these, the Grange, was the home of Sir William Hooker, who was Sheriff of London during the Plague and the Great Fire, and was later Lord Mayor; a summer-house in the grounds carries the date 1672. At the top of Crooms Hill you are outside the west wall of Greenwich Park, with General Wolfe Road dividing the park from Blackheath's gently undulating common. A short distance along Chesterfield Walk, under the wall, you come to the high wrought iron gates of Lord Chesterfield's stately home in which he spent all his summers since he acquired it in the middle of the eighteenth century until he died in 1773. Next-door-neighbour to it, separated by their huge gardens, is Macartney House, now divided into several very attractive flats. Both houses, built into the wall, face one way into Greenwich Park and the other out over Blackheath Common. Both houses are very handsome, but Chesterfield House rather grander. Lord Chesterfield built on the ballroom, with its deep windows at three sides, in 1754. During his lifetime the place was known as Chesterfield House, but in 1815 it became the official residence of the Ranger of Greenwich Park, a post usually held by a member of the royal family, and was known as Ranger's Lodge. Today it is a Community Centre run by the Greater London Council, and in the summer is open for light refreshments; tea on the terrace at the back of the house, facing into the park and overlooking a rose garden, is very pleasant.

But let us return to Observatory Hill to complete our general survey, and this we may do through a small side turning for pedestrians only, leading to an opening in the wall, just before Chesterfield House. Then, with the statue of Wolfe behind us, and the great panorama of London facing us, to the north, and stretching away east and west, let us take a walk eastward across the top of the park, through the huge and ancient sweet-chestnut trees, many of them planted by order of Charles II, their massive ancient trunks twisted at the base into shapes like the legs and feet of elephants, and, passing a pretty little Victorian bandstand, enter some fine flower gardens. These gardens are merely a railed-off section of the park, but whereas out on the hill there is a feeling of wild rural landscape, with grassy hollows and the big old sweet chestnuts and the little twisted hawthorns, here in the formally laid-out gardens there is a sense of graciousness and seclusion, with beautifully kept lawns, sweeping cedar trees, rose-beds, herbaceous borders, an ornamental lake with reeds, willows, ducks, and a rustic bridge. There is also a deer enclosure. Outside on the hill people lie on the grass, and children roll down the slopes and hide in the hollows and play cricket on the level ground in front of the Queen's House, but in the gardens people sit in deck-chairs, or on seats along the paths, where tame squirrels take nuts from the hand. It is lovely outside on the hill, but this is beauty of a different order; that is parkland; this is a garden. The whole park was laid out for Charles II by the great landscape gardener, André Le Nôtre, who designed the gardens of Versailles, Fontainebleau, St. Germain, St. Cloud. The park was 'enstocked' with deer under Queen Elizabeth I.[1]

Unless you know of the existence of the gardens away over beyond the bandstand it is easy to believe that the grassy slopes of Observatory Hill constitute the whole of the royal park.

1. There is a fascinating account of all this in an H.M. Stationery Office publication, *Trees in Greenwich Park*, the Seventh Report of the Advisory Committee on Forestry, 1964.

If you cross the broad avenue which separates these gardens and the main body of the park from the buildings on Observatory Hill you see a large and rather ugly terra-cotta building, known as such, which houses the Caird Planetarium in its dome. If you cut diagonally across the grassy undulations behind you come to the famous Blackheath viewpoint, known as the Point, the view from which is considered by some to be finer than that from the Wolfe statue on Observatory Hill, but with this opinion I emphatically do not agree. It is the panorama commanded by Chesterfield House on the Blackheath side, and his lordship considered it the 'finest prospect in the world'. He liked to watch from his windows 'great merchantmen and frigates of war glide past'. Tragically, at the end of his long life he was blind.

With the memory of Chesterfield watching the river's traffic from the deep windows of his stately home we come back to *maritime* Greenwich and descend the grassy slopes, or traverse the long tree-lined avenue, to the Queen's House, now a part of the National Maritime Museum.

There is a sense in which the whole of Greenwich is a maritime museum, particularly since the *Cutty Sark* was berthed there, to be not only a national monument but itself a museum of maritime treasures. Less than a hundred years ago fishing smacks sailed from Greenwich for the North Sea. In the fourteenth century the chief occupation of the inhabitants of the little but busy town of those days was as watermen. Today there is the busyness of the launches which bring an endless stream of visitors every half an hour down from Westminster, and take them back again, and always the cargo ships hurrying up from the Thames Estuary or slipping down the river on the evening tide to the sea. And, supremely, there is the Royal Naval College and the *Cutty Sark*.

The Queen's House was designed in 1616 by Inigo Jones, for Anne of Denmark, wife of James I, but she died before it was finished, which was not until 1635. It then became the home of Henrietta Maria, the wife of Charles I. It is a small square white palace with a pillared verandah on the first floor. It was an innovation in domestic architecture at that time, being a break-away from the traditional Tudor red brick. It was built to straddle the road, so that the Queen should not have to cross the road to set foot in the park; under the arch, where the road drove under the house, is reputedly the place where Sir Walter Raleigh spread his cloak for Queen Elizabeth I. The colonnades which the visitor sees today mark where the old road ran; they were added in 1807 to commemorate the Battle of Trafalgar, and connect the two wings of the National Maritime Museum, of which the Queen's House is the centre. The road is now nearer the river, leading westward into the town of Greenwich, and eastward thundering out with heavy lorries to Woolwich. On the ground floor of the Queen's House there are Tudor and early Stuart portraits, and paintings of ships of the period. On the first floor there is the Queen's Bedroom with its beautiful painted ceiling, and in her boudoir there is a carved and gilded wooden ceiling made by the crafts-men who constructed the first 'three-decker' ship, *Sovereign of the Seas*, in the same year, 1637. In the centre room, the Bridge Room, there are wonderful models of seventeenth-century sailing ships, exquisitely made to scale in the smallest detail by the shipwrights of the time. In the entrance hall of the house, the Great Hall, a marble floor repeats the pattern of another noble ceiling. The upstairs rooms open off a gallery round this hall. The house is everywhere light and bright from the deep windows, and, its treasures apart, it is well worth visiting for the views from these windows, one way out over the park and Observatory Hill, the other to the domes of the Naval College against the background of river and trees and the old grey city.

The setting of the Queen's House, balanced between the two domed wings of the Royal Naval College, is perfect, whether viewed from the river, with the green hill behind, or from the

hill itself with the river as background, and it is to William and
Mary, and in particular to Queen Mary, that we owe this
perfection. For the explanation it is necessary to go back in
history to the fifteenth century, when Humphrey, Duke of
Gloucester, the brother of Henry V, enclosed the heath land
which is now the park and built a watchtower on the hill to
guard the approaches to London, and a country house beside
the river, which he called Bella Court. The 200 enclosed acres,
which he stocked with deer, was the first of the royal parks. The
twelve-foot brick wall with which James I enclosed the park on
all sides but the north is some two miles long. It cost £2000 to
build, but as it survives to this day the King may be said to have
had his money's worth.

Duke Humphrey had opposed the marriage of his nephew,
Henry VI, to Margaret of Anjou, although he lent them Bella
Court for their honeymoon, and in 1447, two years after the
marriage, he was arrested and imprisoned. He died a few days
later—according to Shakespeare he was murdered. Within
weeks of his death Margaret had taken over Bella Court for
her own. She enlarged it and renamed it the Palace of Plea-
saunce, or Placentia. Here Henry VIII was born and his
daughters, Elizabeth and Mary. In Henry's young manhood
the place really came into its own, with the court frequently in
residence there and pageants and festivities on the grand scale.
With jousting tournaments in the tilt yard, and hunting and
hawking in the park, Greenwich was royal indeed.

James I, however, preferred his new palace at Whitehall,
which is why Inigo Jones designed the small palace, the Queen's
House, for his wife. When her death interrupted the work it
was abandoned. Under the Commonwealth the Tudor palace
of Placentia was allowed to fall into such disrepair that at the
Restoration Charles II demolished it and built a new palace, the
King's House, on the site. The King's extravagances being what
they were money gave out after that and there was no more
building until 1694, under William and Mary, when, as

Frank Carr says,[1] a 'new chapter in the history of Greenwich was opened'. Following the great naval battle of La Hogue, in 1692, the Queen decided that the King's House should be used as a hospital for seamen, like the royal hospital for soldiers which Charles II had established at Chelsea. The great architect of the day, Christopher Wren, was called in to draw up the plans, and proposed to demolish both the King's House and the Queen's House and build the hospital on the cleared site, with a great central dome such as he created for St. Paul's Cathedral. The Queen, however, rejected this grandiose scheme out of hand; she commanded that both the royal houses should be retained, that 'a clearing 115 feet wide be left between the Queen's House and the river to preserve the view; and that the King's House be balanced by a similar building to form the eastward side of what was to become the Grand Square'. The Queen died soon after this but William III had her wishes carried out. The first pensioners arrived in 1705, two years after Queen Anne came to the throne.

In the years of peace that followed the Battle of Waterloo the number of pensioners declined and in 1869 the hospital closed, and in 1873 the Royal Naval College moved from Portsmouth to Greenwich to occupy these noble buildings and become what is virtually the University of the Navy.

The Painted Hall of the King William block—there are three other blocks—is next only to the Sistine Chapel in its nobility of architecture and the richness of its painted ceiling. There are those who rank the ceiling design as greater than Michelangelo's masterpiece. Sir James Thornhill and his assistants worked on it for twenty years, from 1707 to 1727, and certainly it is magnificent. The hall was originally designed as a dining hall for the pensioners, but was apparently only used on special occasions—to eat ordinary meals every day in such splendour would surely be oppressive!—and in 1824 it was converted to use as a picture gallery. In 1937, when the National

1. In *Maritime Greenwich*.

Maritime Museum was opened, and the pictures were transferred to it, the hall became the officers' mess of the Royal Naval College, which it still is. It is open to the public, like the beautiful eighteenth-century chapel in the Queen Mary building, and as with all this 'stately procession of buildings' which form maritime Greenwich there is no charge for admission.

An average of 2000 visitors a day streamed through the turnstiles of the National Maritime Museum in 1964. I have heard the museum referred to as the 'Nelson museum', and it is that, being rich in Nelson relics, but it is very much more: for one thing it contains nearly a thousand items of uniform, 28,000 prints and drawings, 200,000 photographs . . .

Although the buildings which comprise the museum are old, the museum itself was not founded until 1937. The idea of a National Sea Museum, however, goes back to 1910, and the Society for Nautical Research. It was nearly thirty years before the dream could be realised, but it was never abandoned, and step by step it was achieved. Until 1933 the buildings linked by the colonnades were used as the Royal Hospital School, and the Queen's House was used as five residences for the headmaster and members of his staff. When the new school in Suffolk made possible through the generosity of Mr. Gifford Sherman Reade, as an expression of his admiration for the Royal Navy, was completed in 1933, the old buildings, and eleven and a half acres of ground, were freed for the creation of the museum. In 1934 a Bill was introduced into the House of Lords by Earl Stanhope, setting up the National Maritime Museum with a Board of Trustees and a Director. The first Director was the late Sir Geoffrey Callender, Professor of History in the Royal Naval College and for many years the Hon. Secretary of the Society for Nautical Research. Sir James Caird, who had put up most of the money in the 'twenties for the restoration of H.M.S. *Victory*, was to prove a no less wonderful friend to the museum. He had bought and presented to the nation the world-famous Macpherson Collection of maritime pictures, now in the Print Room of the museum, and he bore the whole cost of converting the buildings—over a million and a quarter pounds sterling—and equipping the museum. The Caird Galleries of the west wing are named after him, and the entrance to this wing is known as the Caird entrance. Inside there is an extremely handsome staircase, called the Belfrey Staircase, made from the teak of four old warships. In this wing museum time is kept, ship-fashion, by strokes on the bell of Nelson's ship, *Vanguard*. The Nelson relics are in this wing, and they include the uniform in which he was killed aboard the *Victory* in 1805. In this wing, also, among innumerable other maritime treasures, is the famous painting of Captain Cook by Nathaniel Dance, and, of course, the no less famous painting of the death of Nelson by Lemuel Abbott.

The exhibits in the west wing begin with William and Mary and continue to the end of the Napoleonic Wars in 1815, in the east wing the story is continued to the present day, with the transition from sail to steam in the nineteenth century, and the two world wars of the twentieth continuing England's maritime history.

Extensive as it already is, the museum is growing all the time, and is undoubtedly the most important institution of its kind in existence. Its stated objects are 'to promote and maintain due interest in Seafaring and Shipbuilding, past and present, particularly British, and in Nautical Astronomy. To collect, preserve, study, exhibit, and make available to all who are interested, any objects which will explain the story or assist the student.'

Some facts and figures given me by Mr. Frank Carr concerning this wonderful museum are of interest:

The collection of oil paintings is huge, exceeding in number that of the National Gallery, and included seventeen first-class portraits by Sir Joshua Reynolds. There are more prints and drawings than in the Tate Gallery and the National Portrait

c

Gallery combined. The museum also contains the world's largest and finest collection of the works of marine artists, from the early Dutch masters to the Diploma Collection of the Royal Society of Marine Artists, which continues to expand.

The entire museum is still growing and needs more space. There are already over a mile of galleries, but it is not enough. There are over 11,000 ships' plans, from the late seventeenth century to the present day. The model ships number around a thousand, and there is an immense collection of personal relics, furniture, pottery, silver, glass, and so forth. The manuscripts occupy three-quarters of a mile of shelving, and contain things such as Captain Cook's journals, and Nelson's will.

The library is probably the largest and certainly the finest maritime library in the world.

Flamsteed House, until 1948 the Royal Observatory, became an annexe of the museum, devoted to navigation and astronomy, when the Observatory was re-established at Hurstmonceux Castle, in Sussex, the night skies over London ceasing to be clear enough for astronomical observation. The original observatory came to be called Flamsteed House after the Reverend John Flamsteed, the first Astronomer Royal, appointed by Charles II, who declared by royal warrant on June 22, 1675, that 'in order to the finding out of the longitude of places and for perfecting navigation and astronomy, we have resolved to build a small observatory within our park at Greenwich, upon the highest ground, at or near the place where the castle stood, with lodging rooms for our astronomical observer and assistant'.

Inevitably Sir Christopher Wren, who had by then designed some fifty city churches, including St. Paul's, after the Great Fire, was commissioned to carry out the King's wishes. Always economical, Wren decided to use the foundations of Duke Humphrey's watch-tower to keep down expenses, and the work was carried out for the sum of £500 0s. 1d., raised 'by the sale of decayed gunpowder'.

The Reverend John Flamsteed held the post of 'observator' until his death in 1719, when he was succeeded by Edmond Halley, after whom the comet was named. Flamsteed's story has perhaps no place here, but it was one of dogged struggle— against the ill-health he had known since his youth, against shortage of money—he was obliged to make his own instruments—and against the fierce opposition to his ideas. The interested reader is referred to Francis Baily's *Account of the Reverend John Flamsteed* (1835), compiled from an autobiographical narrative and numerous letters, which is still the leading authority for his life.

The beautiful Octagon Room, with its deep windows, at the centre of Flamsteed House, was Flamsteed's 'Camera Stellata', and this has been restored as far as possible to its original state, with replicas of the clocks by Thomas Tompion, the 'father of English watch-making', who died in 1713. The rooms below, in which Flamsteed lived, have been refurnished with period pieces, and the rest of the building, which is on different levels, together with the Meridian Building to the south, opened in 1967, have been arranged into twelve galleries named after Astronomers Royal, with one for Sir William Herschel who designed and made the forty-foot reflecting telescope with the four-foot mirror, which is one of the treasures of Flamsteed House.

Flamsteed House was opened to the public in 1960, and even for those who know nothing about astronomy and are not particularly interested in it, it is a delightful place to visit, for the charm of the rooms, and the views out over London one way and the green wooded hill of the park the other, and outside you can check your watch by Greenwich Mean Time.

And then, finally, the lovely ship, the *Cutty Sark*, dominating maritime Greenwich.

There are, I suppose, for everyone certain sights which lift up the heart, by their sheer beauty, or by sentimental association. In the days when islanders, such as the English, travelled to foreign countries over the sea instead of through the air, the first glimpse of the 'white cliffs of Dover' on the return journey could move the voyager to tears; I do not know whether a similar emotion is evoked for the modern traveller by the first sight of London Airport—that it doesn't thus affect me proves nothing except my detestation of air-travel. For me the authentic thrill, the ecstatic lift of the heart, is provided by the first glimpse of the tall masts of the *Cutty Sark*, berthed by Greenwich Pier, as you come down the river from Westminster. I have made the trip many times, but every time I am impelled to exclaim to my companion, rapturously, 'Ah, there she is! The *Cutty Sark*!' As though I had never seen her before, and as though my companion cannot see for him- or herself. Those who share my love for her will understand. A thing of beauty is a joy forever, and its loveliness increases—and re-asserts itself—at every viewing.

Frank Carr writes lyrically of her in his *Maritime Greenwich*: 'How perfectly she fits into the Greenwich scene, this last survivor of the splendid tea clippers that a hundred years ago distinguished the golden age of sail.' Alan Villiers subtitles his book, *The Cutty Sark*, 'Last of a Glorious Era', and writing of her says 'the last of a glorious era, indeed she is, and one of the noblest of them all'.

It is fitting that her final berth should be at Greenwich, for although she was launched on the Clyde, on November 23, 1869, built by Scottish shipbuilders for a Scotsman, Captain John Willis, 'Old White Hat', or 'White Hat Willis', as he was called, from the white top hat he affected, she was registered in London, where her owner had settled, and London was her home port until 1895. 'Cutty sark' is Scots dialect for short shirt, or chemise, and the expression occurs in Burns' poem, *Tam O'Shanter*:

Whene'r to drink you are inclined
Or Cutty Sarks run in your mind ...

Whatever the reason which would account for Captain
Willis' quirk in naming his new crack clipper ship *Cutty Sark*
it was his business, and the secret—if it was that—has died with
him. For the ship's figurehead he had the famous craftsman,
Robert Hellyer, of Blackwall, carve the witch, Nannie, from
Burns' poem, pursuing with one arm outstretched the fleeing
Tam, and on the ship's bows he had Hellyer carve a frieze of
naked witches dancing in support of Nannie, but these were
removed before the ship went into the Australian wool trade.
The outstretched arm was washed away and replaced several
times, and eventually the head of the witch herself; it, too, was
replaced, but not by a craftsman of Hellyer's calibre, and the
existing head is not lovely, as was the original, but fiendish;
the present figurehead is new, having been carved as recently
as 1957.

The *Cutty Sark* was designed to gain for her owner the blue
riband of the sea of those days by winning the annual tea race
home from China, but in this she was beaten by the *Thermopylae*. She was anyhow too late for the tea trade, for the Suez
Canal opened the trade to steamships a week before she was
launched, and from 1885 to 1895 she was on the Australian run
as a wool clipper, under her most famous master, Captain
Richard Woodget. Villiers says of him that he was a 'great
shipmaster', adding that 'he deserved the *Cutty Sark*, and the
Cutty Sark deserved him', and that he could think of no finer
compliment to either. Captain Woodget was a 'driver', and
under him the *Cutty Sark* was never beaten by another ship
on the homeward run.

She had other great captains, and not least of them the
unfortunate Captain J. S. Wallace in 1878, who went over the
side of the ship after tragic happenings on board in 1880. It was

what Basil Lubbock, the great historian of the *Cutty Sark*, called a 'hell ship voyage',[1] and, for what it's worth, Wallace defied an old tradition of the sea by sailing on a Friday.

The *Cutty Sark* had two more captains and many voyages and troubles after that before she came under the command of Captain Woodget in 1885; one was a disaster, and the less said about him the better; the other, Captain E. Moore, was a very good captain indeed, and 'Old White Hat' was delighted, after his spell of bad luck with poor Wallace and his bad-lot successor. Captain Moore took over the ship when she was in very poor shape, and Willis was not inclined to spend much money on her, but the new captain was a first-class seaman, and the first time he commanded her he spent almost the entire voyage getting her properly seaworthy again. He took her on two voyages, in 1883 and 1884 to Australia, in the wool trade, very successfully, showing what she could do in the great winds off Cape Horn and the great seas of the Roaring Forties for which she had never been designed or intended. Her owner, who had begun to lose interest in her, discovered a new pride in her; in 1883 she made the fastest passage of the year; she had not won him the blue riband of the sea in the tea trade, but as a wool clipper she was the fastest ship afloat—and speed meant money; it was the fast ship that got the cargoes, and it was an era of increasing competition. In her middle age the *Cutty Sark* had come into her own at last.

After his two highly successful Australian runs Captain Moore was promoted to the flagship of the Willis fleet, and the forty-year-old Captain Richard Woodget, who had served with Willis since 1881, was appointed to the *Cutty Sark*. He was, quite simply, a magnificent seaman, and he took her on some remarkable runs during the next ten years. He made her, says Alan Villiers, in his book about her, a 'queen of the sea'. But 'White Hat' Willis was a business man, and even a ship that could make the fastest passage of the season as a clipper

1. In an appendix to his famous *Log of the Cutty Sark*, 1945.

could not compete as a paying proposition with the ships with a bigger cargo space, and with the advent of the steamship—and with the Suez Canal, which Willis had by then given up hoping would cave in. When Woodget got back to London in record time with a record cargo from Sydney he learned that Willis was negotiating the sale of the ship to two brothers named Ferreira and the deal went through. Willis gave Woodget another ship, but he only made one voyage in her; his heart was in the *Cutty Sark*, and he retired from the sea to Norfolk, where he was born, and became a farmer, like his father, and he died there in 1928, at the age of eighty-two.

But the end of his life had the crowning glory of once more boarding the beloved ship and steering her, for a time, under tow from Falmouth to Fowey, for a regatta in 1924. For twenty-nine years he had not set eyes on her, and then as an old man to board her again, the gallant old ship, and feel the wheel again under his hands, and see her again restored to her youthful beauty . . . we can only conjecture his emotions, and be glad, that so late in the day, he was vouchsafed the reunion.

The Portuguese owners changed her name to *Ferreira*, under which name she roamed the ports of the world until 1922—in the last few months under yet another name, *Maria do Ampara*, having been sold again. It is interesting that when the Ferreiras had her she was still *El Pequina Camisola* to her crew.

Then in 1922 Captain Wilfred Dowman came upon her in Falmouth Harbour, where she had had to run for shelter from bad weather. He had once been passed by her at sea, homeward-bound from Sydney in 1894, when she was under the command of Captain Woodget and in fine trim. Now, down-and-out and neglected, and under the name of *Maria do Ampara*, she was still recognisable to her old admirer. The Captain's shocked excitement must have been considerable, for he made inquiries and discovered that her Portuguese owners would only be too glad to sell her, since she no longer paid her way, but she had to

complete her voyage back to Lisbon. When she had done so
Captain Dowman had her towed back to Falmouth. It was, as
Alan Villiers says in his book about her, 'a great gesture,
worthy of the ship and of the best of shipmasters'.

Captain Dowman restored and re-rigged the old ship and
put her to use as a training-ship for boys intending careers in
the merchant service. It had been his dream to give her a new
suit of sails and send her to sea again, but he died in 1937 before
the dream could be realised. His widow, who shared his love
for the *Cutty Sark*, presented her to the Thames Nautical
Training College, and in 1938 she was towed from Falmouth to
the Thames, where she was moored close to the training ship,
Worcester, off Greenhithe.

She survived the war, just as she had come unscathed through
the First World War, for all her roaming of the seas. After the
Second World War she was no longer needed as a training ship
and in 1949 she was offered as a gift to the National Maritime
Museum—but the trustees of the museum had neither the
power nor the resources for the preservation of the ship. It was
then that the Duke of Edinburgh, himself a trustee, came to the
rescue, and at his instigation a committee was formed, out of
which emerged the Cutty Sark Society in 1952, under the
chairmanship of Mr. Henry Barraclough, M.V.O., with the
Duke as patron, and on May 28, 1953, at Greenhithe, His
Royal Highness accepted the ship on behalf of the Society. The
London County Council provided a site by Greenwich Pier,
and on December 10, 1954, the *Cutty Sark* moved into the
specially built dry dock. On June 25, 1957, Her Majesty the
Queen went to Greenwich to declare the ship open to the
public.

That is the story of the home-coming of the *Cutty Sark* in
brief; the restoration of the ship to her original condition as a
crack clipper ship of the tea trade of 1869 is a story in itself.
This tremendous task was carried out by Sir Joseph Rawlinson,

the chief engineer of the L.C.C., and his staff. In a paper written
and presented to the Royal Institution of Naval Architects at
their Spring Meeting in 1965, Frank Carr recounted for the
first time the whole fascinating story of how the 'bits and
pieces of the *Cutty Sark* jig-saw puzzle were assembled from all
over the world', until there were enough to restore and re-rig
the ship as she was in her heyday. Mr. Carr was chairman of the
technical and rigging committees that did the work, and is now
chairman of the Ship Management Committee that runs the
ship. For those interested, the paper has been reprinted as a
pamphlet by the Cutty Sark Society.

By 1964 the two millionth visitor had been received on
board the *Cutty Sark*. Today, the valiant little clipper who
found it increasingly difficult to earn her keep at sea earns it
now in dry dock in her final berth.

On a plaque at one end of the dock is inscribed: *Here to
commemorate an era, the* Cutty Sark *has been preserved as a tribute
to the ships and men of the merchant navy in the days of sail'*, and
there follow two lines from Masefield's poem, *Ships:*

> They mark our passage as a race of men
> Earth will not see such ships as these again.

It is a fine and moving experience to tread the deck of the
Cutty Sark, to look up at her tall masts and see the London sky
and the trees of Greenwich waterfront through the delicate
intricacies of her rigging . . . nearly two miles of wire, and ten
of cordage, for those who like statistics. You may peep into the
crew's quarters and see how small were the cabins that housed
six men or more, and how short and narrow the berths with
their straw-filled 'donkey' mattresses. In this confined space
there is still room for a narrow plank table with a narrow bench
each side of it. Below, aft, are the officers' quarters, the cabins
rather larger, but still cramped; there is a saloon with an oil
lamp swinging from the ceiling, and, astonishingly, an open

fireplace, with a mantel over, disconcerting in its Victorian domesticity. In the galley there is a replica of the original black iron stove, and imagination boggles at the thought of cooking meals on it as the ship plunged and rolled down in the Roaring Forties.

In the 'tween decks, where you go in, tea-chests are stowed at one side, and bales of wool at the other, illustrating the ship's history as a tea clipper and an Australian wool ship. There are some fine prints of sailing ships and models of sailing ships, including Sir Maurice Denny's wonderful model of the *Cutty Sark*, considered to be the finest clipper ship model in the world. It is exquisite in its delicate precision, and very beautiful. All this part of the ship is a maritime museum of very great interest. There are some faded photographs of Captain Woodget, and some pages from his log. In the lower hold there are fifty merchant ship figureheads, from the 'Long John Silver' collection.

'Long John Silver', as most school-children know, was a swashbuckling sea-captain, with a patch over one eye, in *Treasure Island*. But the Captain 'Long John' Silver who presented this remarkable collection of figureheads to the *Cutty Sark* was a London business man, Mr. Sydney Cumbers, a printing-ink manufacturer by profession but a seaman by inclination. His boyhood ambition to go to sea was frustrated by the loss of one eye caused by an accident with a toy gun when he was ten years old, and the frustration if anything intensified his longing. The manufacture of printing ink proving lucrative he was able to indulge a hobby in which his frustration was sublimated on an heroic scale. In his house, which he called the Look-Out, overlooking the river at Gravesend, he enacted the part of a merchant sea-captain with such intensity and consistency that Captain 'Long John' Silver, as he called himself in this role—he called it his *nom de mer*—became in a sense more real than the business man who was Mr. Sydney Cumbers. He dressed like a sea-captain, wearing a reefer jacket and a peaked

cap with an immaculately white cover, and over his injured eye
he wore a black patch. His house was virtually a ship; the
Quarterly Review of the Royal Naval Benevolent Trust, for
Winter 1952, entitled an article about it 'M.V. *Look-Out*', and a
writer in *La Revue Maritime Belge, Wanderlaer et sur l'eau*, for
January, 1950, said of it that it looked like a ship, sounded like a
ship, and felt like a ship.

The house is now part of a hotel, so that the detailed description given in the *Quarterly Review* is of value: 'The front door
opens on to the Main Gangway, complete with deckrails and
lifebelts, and on the starboard side is the Hurricane deck, whilst
the Fo'c'sle, Well, Half- and Quarter-decks are to port, a ladder
leads to "B" deck, where the Bridge and Charthouse are situated. There are gratings, ventilators and scuttles, and the deck
of the Bridge is laid with planking from the *Neuralia*. The Seth
Thomas clock strikes bells to mark the hours and half-hours in
nautical fashion . . . The walls and ceiling of the Bridge, which
looks out over the Thames, are painted to give the impression of
sea and sky. With the exception of a dummy funnel, the
semaphore and the morse-lamp, which came from the last
pre-war Shipping Exhibition, everything on the Bridge has
been taken from a sea-going ship and is at least fifty years
old. The masthead light came from the first hospital ship
Maine and the ship's bell is that of the old *Mauretania*. The
lifeboats, which appear to be whole, are actually halves
mounted on mirrors, the reflections serving to complete the
illusion. It needs but slight imagination, when standing at
the wheel with the engine-room telegraph at "Full Ahead",
to believe that the Look-Out is steaming down the Thames
bound foreign in search of more items for her owner's
collection.'

Visitors to the Look-Out were always invited in a nautical
bellow to 'Come aboard'; this would be followed by a shrill
whistle. His attractive and charming wife was always referred
to as the 'Mate'. In the correct Long John Silver tradition his flag

was the Jolly Roger—and he kept it flying for twenty-one years.

But more important than all this elaborate make-believe is the fact that in those twenty-one years at the Look-Out he assembled an important and unique private maritime museum. The most interesting of his treasures was a remarkable collection of 101 merchant ships' figureheads, the largest in the world. In the course of time his museum became world-famous and a day rarely passed without visitors, very many of whom were the officers of ships that put into the Port of London. The purser of one of the Swedish-Lloyd ships liked to bring over parties of passengers in the ferry to Gravesend for them to meet the 'Captain' and see the museum. 'Captain' was a courtesy title given him as of right by his numerous and faithful admirers in and around the Port of London; nobody knew Mr. Sydney Cumbers; everyone knew the 'Cap'n'. Outside of the business world he was never known by any other name than Captain Silver; in the Members' List of the Society for Nautical Research his name appears as Silver, not Cumbers.

In the small waterside garden of the Look-Out he put up a flagmast from which he could make signals to passing ships in the International Code. He was fortunate in that the 'Mate' was entirely sympathetic to all these nautical activities and shared fully in the excitement, interest and 'fun'—it is her word—of collecting for the museum. When the figureheads needed repainting it was she who did it, and it was she who with the minimum of help kept the glass cases and the entire museum immaculately dusted. Everything about the 'M.V. Look-Out' was kept *ship*-shape.

The Look-Out adjoined the Clarendon Hotel, to which it belonged, and in 1952 the proprietors wanted to take over the house for the purpose of making a new American bar and restaurant. With his ship threatened and with nowhere suitable to house his by then considerable collection of figureheads and nautical relics Captain Silver offered it to the Corporation of Gravesend, but they, also, had nowhere to house a maritime

museum; in retrospect the obvious thing would seem to have
been to have accepted the collection and stored it pending the
acquisition of suitable premises, but indecisions and delays lost
the collection for Gravesend, because whilst all the shilly-
shallying was going on the Cutty Sark Society had been
formed to restore and exhibit the ship and Mr. Cumbers, for
whom the matter of rehousing his museum was urgent,
offered the whole collection to the Society—which immediately and gratefully accepted the splendid gift. General Sir
Frederick Browning (late husband of Daphne du Maurier)
went down to Gravesend to take over the collection on behalf
of the Duke of Edinburgh.

In the first annual report of the Cutty Sark Society, for the
year 1953, the following record of the gift appears:

'The Board has all along intended to use *Cutty Sark* not
only as a sentimental memorial to the Merchant Navy, but also
to serve a useful purpose as a "live" ship, which can be used in
many practical ways, in addition to becoming a focal point
upon which to base various educational activities. Thus, a
Museum, consisting of objects of maritime interest of all kinds,
will be set up in the vessel. In this connection the Board has been
fortunate indeed in having received, as a gift, the well-known
collection owned by Captain "Long John" Silver, a pseudonym
which hides the identity of a London business man. This
comprises some 750 exhibits of great interest, of which 101 are
ships' figureheads, an unparalleled gathering of those intrig-
uing adornments to ships that went down to the sea in the days
of sail.'

Only thirty-eight of the figureheads are at present exhibited
in the lower hold of the *Cutty Sark*, the remainder being in
store for the time being, together with the bulk of the collection of models, relics, documents and the like, from which a
selection of items is exhibited on board, with changes and
additions continually being made to maintain and vary the
interest as much as possible.

Captain Silver found his figureheads over the course of years in breakers' yards and in villages off coasts notorious for wrecks, where he would find them decorating gardens and negotiate for them. One he found in a village only ten miles from Gravesend. Where possible he traced the history of each figurehead—the name and character of the ship, its nationality, what happened to it, when and where it was wrecked. Some of the figureheads are beautiful, some are grotesque, others are ugly. Some have been roughly carved by local craftsmen and have little artistic merit; others suggest the work of artists, and one, the beautiful *Golden Cherubs*, has been attributed to the famous woodcarver, Grinling Gibbons, though recent investigations cast doubt on the likelihood of this. It is believed to be the oldest British merchant-ship figurehead in existence.

The beautiful white *Lady of the Rose* is from an unknown ship, possibly a French nitrate ship wrecked off the Norfolk coast. The figurehead was found in a dilapidated condition in a wood yard at Wisbech, Cambridgeshire. A fine gilded eagle was the figurehead of a full-rigged ship, *Eagle*, built in 1856 at Bristol. A young woman wearing a blue dress with a green, buckled belt, and holding a red rose, is from a 540-ton barque built at Sunderland in 1864. She was named *Bertha Marion* after the owner's daughter, whom the figurehead represents. In 1879 she was sold to a company which ran the ARA Line and was renamed *Aralura*. She was sold again in 1890 to Norway and was renamed *Beda*, after the Norwegian goddess. There is a little grey figure of *Florence Nightingale* as a young woman, from a schooner which traded in the Mediterranean. An interesting and attractive figurehead of a girl wearing a green skirt with a low-cut brown bodice, and with hair reaching to her shoulders, is believed to be from the ship called *Diana* built at Northfleet in Kent, in 1799, and which went to the Arctic in search of Sir John Franklin's North-West Passage expedition which was lost in 1848. The figurehead was found in a gar-

den at Bean, in Kent. A large Oriental beauty is the figure
of a China tea clipper called *Lalla Rooke* built at Liverpool
in 1856. This 869-ton ship went ashore in a dense fog on
the rocks at Gammon Head, near Prawle Point, Devon, in
1873, after a voyage on which she had covered 3000 miles.
The figurehead was found in Jersey and was brought to
England just before the Second World War. The figurehead
of the *Augusta Louise*, which was wrecked off the Orkneys,
was found at Kirkwell. There is a small figurehead of *General
Gordon*, from a brigantine, and a similarly small one from
a brig called the *Omar Pasha*, built in 1854, a little ship of
only 225 tons. The figurehead was found in Malta, and is
unusual in having glass eyes. A fine Red Indian figure, with
feathered head-dress and a pipe of peace at the side, is from a
steel ship, *Hiawatha*, of 1490 tons, built at Dumbarton in 1891
for a Norwegian owner. She was sold in Norway in 1917
and renamed *Fiskjo*, and was broken up at a yard in Devon
in 1924.

My favourite is a nude white Aphrodite, her lower half
modestly and gracefully clad in green leaves; she is very
beautiful, but her history is not known. They are all, even the
most primitive and unaesthetic, evocative of the dead-and-gone
ships whose prows they decorated, and some of which did
heroic journeys like the *Cutty Sark* herself and on the last
voyage did not reach port. Such cruel seas, those figureheads
have known, such mountainous waves and driving rains, and
the ports of the world in another age, and such blistering
suns.

So many times have I been down into the hold of the
Cutty Sark and renewed acquaintance with those wooden
relics of the great days of sail, always with pleasure and interest—and emotion; but not until I began writing this book did I
realise my indebtedness to that great Thamesman, Captain
'Long John' Silver. I wonder, now, how many do realise this indebtedness, as they wander from figurehead to figurehead,

pausing to read the legend below which so often recounts a
wreck?

The hobby through which Sydney Cumbers overcame the
frustration imposed by a boyhood mishap has enriched
maritime Greenwich and the lovely ship which is her pride, and
has afforded interest and delight to men, women and children
of all nationalities for many years, and will continue to do so
for as long as London's old grey river flows down past Greenwich to the sea.

God bless Captain Silver!

In 1964 the Advisory Committee on Forestry, appointed by
the Ministry of Public Building and Works, in its Report on
Greenwich Park, recommended that hawthorn trees on the
grassy slopes of Observatory Hill, being 'insufficiently formal
for this position', should 'in due course be renewed, perhaps
with holly, which would give an ultimate height of less than
thirty feet but would be sufficiently architectural to connect
the upper to the lower landscape'. Ah, the little twisted
hawthorn trees, white with blossom in the sweet month of
May—who would wish to lie beneath an architectural holly
tree instead? Who would even wish to sit on a seat in front of
Wolfe's statue and look down on tall dark holly trees instead
of friendly little hawthorn trees? Alas, and alas; and alas for the
graceful cedars which give such distinction to the flower
gardens, for the gentlemen of the advisory committee recommend that 'the young cedars planted in recent years should
be removed, together with the older specimens as these become unsightly'. They suggest that they be replaced 'with one
or two specimens of sorbus, mulberry or tulip trees as appropriate'.

Less alarming is the proposal to restore the giant grass steps
on Observatory Hill, with some hard steps at the side . . . and
sliding on the grass steps to be discouraged ('there are plenty of
sliding slopes adjoining'). In the early eighteenth century, the

report tells us, in an historical note, rolling down Observatory Hill was 'an essential part of the merriment' in the park, 'twice a year at least, at the time of the Greenwich Fair'.

The Committee appreciates 'that use of a much-frequented public park is very different from that in the seventeenth century', but nevertheless they feel that 'the restoration of the giant grass steps is of the first importance and strongly recommend that it should be carried out'. The object is to 'restore the plan of the park as nearly as possible to the layout shown in the seventeenth-century print. . . .'

'Greenwich Park', declares the Report, 'is still potentially the finest interpretation in England of a layout based on that grand seventeenth-century conception of design that governed also the grouping of the buildings leading to the river.' For this reason they recommend that 'this unique seventeenth-century formal layout' be restored 'to the original condition which has been exactly recorded in a contemporary print'. They attribute the present state of the park to 'the neglect of the eighteenth century, to the contrary ideas of the nineteenth century and to the consequence of its use as a Public Park . . . Most old prints since 1700 indicate the decay in formality, and it may be that this gradual change is characteristic of the English temperament.'

But isn't change characteristic of civilised life everywhere? Blackheath is no longer a wild heath, and motor cars in an endless stream at weekends come down Duke Humphreys Road and into the park; Flamsteed House is no longer the habitation of the observator, and the Observatory is no longer an observatory but a museum; Macartney House has been made into flats, and the *hoi-polloi* can partake of tea and light refreshments in what was once the stately home of Lord Chesterfield. The *Cutty Sark* no longer sails the seas and you can buy picture postcards on board. In the Queen's House people stand about with ear-phones on their heads listening intently to a recorded talk telling them all about it. And on summer nights *son et*

D

lumiére brings the centuries of history to life. Why should the park, then, be restored to seventeenth-century formality, now in the late twentieth? In that restored landscape, it is pertinent to ask, what becomes of the twentieth-century litter bins? Aesthetically they should be abolished, but practically that would be a pity, for human nature being what it is the need is not for their abolition for but more of them.

Perhaps the Committee's recommendations will never be carried out. If they are, will we who love Greenwich Park, and all that is part of it, like it? Will we feel at home there, any more . . . with the dark formal holly trees?

Greenwich Park has always been subject to change, as far back as the end of the seventeenth century, when royalty moved away and the Observatory was built, and the Royal Palace became a Naval hospital. Pensioners would have walked in the park then, and by the eighteenth century the general public were enjoying themselves rolling down the slopes.

Dr. Johnson had 'country lodgings' for a time in Greenwich, and composed his poem, *Irene*, under the trees in the park. In the summer of 1763 he revisited it with Boswell. 'Come,' said he (Boswell records), 'let us make a day of it and go down to Greenwich to dine.' They went by river, and two days later they went to Billingsgate and hired a rowing-boat and rowed to Greenwich, and were 'charmed with the beautiful fields on each side of the river'. At Greenwich Boswell 'felt great pleasure in being at the place which Mr. Johnson celebrates in his *London: a Poem*'. On this occasion Johnson observed that the building at Greenwich was 'too magnificent for a place of charity, and too much detached to make one great whole'. They returned to London by water in the evening, and it was chilly, and Boswell was glad to get back to the 'warm comfort' of London. Boswell, anyhow, considered the park 'not equal to Fleet Street'. He was the inveterate Londoner and not happy for long away from it.

Finally, no account of maritime Greenwich is complete

without mention of the whitebait dinners held at the Old Ship Hotel which stood near the pier. It was bombed during the Second World War and the dry dock for the *Cutty Sark* was built on the site. The Trafalgar Tavern, the rival of the Ship, was older, and, of course, still exists; a ministerial whitebait dinner was held there in 1859, on August 10, two days before the end of the Parliamentary session. Lord Palmerston and his cabinet liked to dine at the Ship Tavern, and contemplating the whitebait on one occasion is said to have suggested to his colleagues, 'Let us all imitate this very wise little fish—and drink a lot and say nothing.' Disraeli and his cabinet attended a whitebait dinner there on September 1st, 1880, going by river from Westminster pier. Lord Rosebery attended a whitebait dinner, one of the last, in 1895.

Charles Dickens knew and loved Greenwich, and in his novel, *Our Mutual Friend*, describes a wedding dinner there 'in a little room overlooking the river', where everything was delightful—'The Park was delightful; the dishes of fish were delightful; the wine was delightful.' He himself gave a dinner there to celebrate the publication of *Martin Chuzzlewit*.

It is still all delightful, and though the old Ship Tavern is no longer there the old ship *Cutty Sark* graces the spot, and, despite all the changes, the view from the river is unchanged from when Canaletto painted it in the mid-eighteenth century. And the painting itself is in the Queen's House, and across from it the lovely painting, all warm golds and ambers and browns, of the Queen's House and the King's House, said to have been done to the order of Samuel Pepys, by Hendrik Danckerts. With his naval associations maritime Greenwich would have had a natural appeal for Pepys. He, also, was a born and bred Londoner—and he died at Clapham.

3

Gravesend and the Cap'n's Widow

When Mr. and Mrs. Cumbers had to leave the Look-Out they were fortunate in finding a tall old house lying back on a low ridge a few yards from it. It was a very dilapidated old house, and from the photographs Mrs. Cumbers showed me, of the exterior and interior, before the restoration it seemed that only an act of great faith could envisage anything congenial emerging from such chaos. The restoration—the house was practically gutted—took two years, during which time the captain and the mate lived in a flat in London, and instead of the shipping of the Thames Estuary the ex-master of 'M.V. Look-Out' had only the traffic swirling round Hyde Park to look at. There were frequent trips to Gravesend, to be sure, to supervise the work of Thames House —Look-Out number two—but it was not the same as living day and night within sight and sound of the Thames shipping, watching the ebb and flow of the tides, having the skippers from cargo ships call when they put into the Port of London, running up messages on his flagstaff to passing ships. The captain was 'lost'. And then, on the very day when the house was finally finished, he was struck down by a stroke which paralysed him all down one side and impaired his speech—he who had always been such a great talker.

He had his own special sanctum at the top of the house, itself a small maritime museum, and commanding a magnificent view, but he spent his days sitting in an armchair at the dining-room window on the ground floor, the stairs being many and steep. Mrs. Cumbers showed me the house, and at the end, sadly, the 'Captain's chair'. If I, who had never met him, could imagine him sitting there, what was it for her?

But Lois Cumbers is a woman of courage and character— she had to be the last not merely to live with a man as indivi-dual and dynamic as the Cap'n but to find it fun. 'He was *fun*!' she said to me, reciting some of his quips; she didn't say it ruefully, but warmly, appreciatively, the memory of it all still strongly with her. 'He had a good life,' she said, and, with zest in her own voice, 'He had such a feeling for life.'

She looked so pretty and feminine in her heliotrope-coloured dress and pearls, sitting in her be-cushioned and be-flowered drawing room, that I asked her hadn't it sometimes been a little trying living in a house that was virtually a ship; she replied that oh, no, she had had her own room, she had insisted on that, and the 'ship' kept out of the kitchen. Life had its difficulties, all the same, for, she told me, they seldom sat down to lunch together, because every day there would be visitors; she would set his lunch aside for him but usually it was 'stone cold' before he reached it—but it didn't matter to him; he ate it all up barely noticing what he ate; he wasn't interested in food but in ships and ships' captains and people who took an intelligent interest in his museum. If he were at sea he couldn't be particular as to what time he ate, or what, and to all intents and purposes he was at sea in the 'M.V. Look-Out'.

He died in London in 1959 at the age of eighty-three and was buried there. Sentimentally one could have wished he could have been buried at Gravesend, but his real life ended there years before, when the 'M.V. Look-Out' was broken up and he had parted with his wonderful collection of ships' figureheads.

I was glad to have visited Mrs. Cumbers at Gravesend instead of at the flat in London, because although the Cap'n was gone I wanted to see the view that meant so much to him, and, secondarily, I was interested to see Gravesend, having a feeling for these old Thames Estuary places—and Gravesend is very old, being recorded in the Domesday Book as Gravesham, though it has been suggested that the name derives from Greaves End. It is the entrance to the Port of London, and all shipping must stop there, to pick up the river pilot and to present a clean bill of health. A 'hythe' or landing place is mentioned in the Domesday survey. The first Queen Elizabeth established Gravesend as the point at which distinguished visitors would be received and escorted up the river in a state procession. There were also processions down the river, the sad processions of the convicts being exiled to Botany Bay. That good Quaker, Elizabeth Fry, would go out to the prison ships to hand in bundles of coloured squares of cloth for the wretched men to stitch into quilts so that when they arrived at the other side of the world, months later, they had something to sell. With her crusading zeal for prison reform she tried, also, to improve conditions on these grim transports.

There is a fishing fleet off Gravesend, their rust-coloured sails bringing colour to the grey river with its endless busy procession upstream and down, of tugs and lighters, and barges and cargo boats; the fishing boats get shrimps from the sandbanks off the coast between Gravesend and Harwich, and are known as 'Bawley boats', from the boiler in which the shrimps are cooked.

I liked Gravesend, with its narrow streets running down to the waterfront, once you have crossed the modern main street, which is a shopping thoroughfare like any other, and I was delighted when hurrying on down to the river suddenly to glimpse in a church yard a bronze statue which, with a feather standing upright at the back of the head, looked uncommonly like an American Indian figure. I knew that the Indian chieftain's daughter, Pocahontas, who died in a ship off Gravesend whilst preparing to return home after a visit to England in

1617, was buried in Gravesend, and had intended going in search of the grave when I left Mrs. Cumbers, but there she was, presented to me without any searching, in the graveyard of St. George's Church. It is a pleasant bronze of a young girl with her hands at her sides, the palms turned outwards, faintly supplicating, and she looks out to the river. Whether a Red Indian girl of the seventeenth century would have worn a short dress as depicted in the statue seems open to question, for even today when the American Indian women wear national dress their long full skirts reach gracefully to the ground. But there she is, with only her name on the granite pedestal. There would appear to be some doubt as to whether she did in fact save John Smith, the coloniser of Virginia, from death at the hands of her father's tribe but it is a romantic legend. She married John Rolfe, one of the Virginian colonists, and was the first of her tribe to become a Christian. There is no mention of her intervention in Smith's own narratives written at the time, or in the chronicles of his friends, and it has been suggested that the story was invented in *Generall Historie*, published in 1624, seven years after her death, to romanticise the beautiful young Indian 'princess' who was such a social success in England and who died in such tragic circumstances in her youth. I can find no reference to her in various authoritative works on the American Indians. But I am glad Gravesend honours her memory, and I am glad to have seen her memorial statue.

I observed a great many sikhs in Gravesend, shivering without overcoats in the cold March wind, and I observed some public gardens made from an old graveyard, where the last crocuses lingered in the grass.

In the train, trundling back across the grey wastes of the Kent marshes, all chimneys and factories, industrialisation in all its brutal ugliness, it was heartening to see again the tall spars of the lovely ship, the *Cutty Sark*, rising gracefully above maritime Greenwich, redeeming all the ugliness that had gone before, and the Deptford dreariness to come.

I was glad to have made the dreary journey to Gravesend and met the Cap'n's gallant widow, and looked on the splendid panorama of shipping in the Thames Estuary, which was so major a part of the Cap'n's life, and which is so traditional a part of the English scene. He called it Bawley Bay, and declared that if he didn't know it was Gravesend he'd say it was Cornwall. . . .[1]

1. Recorded in a chapter entitled 'Long John Silver', in a book by James A. Jones, *The Romance of London's River*, 1935. The author went aboard the *Look-Out* at Gravesend with a pilot called Captain Weir. He describes Captain Silver as stalking his bridge like a buccaneer. 'He acted the part all right. That lean figure and that black patch, and the harsh emphasis of his voice, and the jocose tyranny of his words—what else could you call him but Captain Long John Silver?'

4

Guildford and the Surrey Hills

M y father, who claimed that he was a Cockney because he was born in the City of Westminster in which, he insisted, you could hear Bow bells when the wind was in the right direction, became in the course of years very weary of going every day, sometimes seven times a week, to the city to sort letters at Mount Pleasant G.P.O., and he would look across the dense roof-tops of south London to a distant blue ridge he said was the Surrey hills and declare, 'some day those hills are going to get me'. By which we children understood that one day Father intended to go on strike, and instead of going to work, 'to earn the money to buy bread to keep up the strength to go to work to earn the money to buy the bread', as he was fond of saying, would play truant and make for the hills and fields of the countryside. He never did, of course, though he reiterated the assertion down through the years, and no doubt the fantasy kept him going the forty years he had to work before his retirement at the age of sixty.

When I was fifteen and doing the monotonous daily trek to an office myself I had great sympathy with my father, and I, too, would look across to that distant blue ridge and indulge the fantasy of playing truant ... and like my father I never did; but then, mercifully, I had only five years of office life and the daily train. I wondered about those Surrey hills though; where exactly were they? How did you get to them?

Well, said my father, there was the Hog's Back at Guildford, wasn't there, and Box Hill, near Dorking, and there was Epsom Downs, wasn't there? Very nice walking there was on Epsom Downs, and there was Holmbury Hill, and Pitch Hill, and Leith Hill—they were further out; but Box Hill and Epsom Downs, they were very nice and handy.

Box Hill, when I was fifteen, was my first Surrey hill; I was taken there one Saturday afternoon—people worked Saturday mornings at their offices in those days—by an artist who was in the art department of the advertising agency in which I was a junior typist. We went by train to a little country station plainly marked Box Hill, and crossed a country road and climbed up steeply behind a small roadside pub, and when we reached the top we sat on the chalky ridge and looked down on little scrubby hawthorn trees, and out across a splendid view, and it was all new and exciting, and real *country*, and an experience to be repeated. We went, too, to Epsom Downs, which was, as my father had said, very nice walking, and Epsom a quiet little country town.

In half a century Box Hill is unchanged, except that there are more people on it—not ramblers, as walkers were once called, nor hikers, as they came later to be called, but people who have got out of their cars and toiled up for the view, and who, when they have seen it, and recovered their breath, gratefully make the descent back to their cars. The old-style walker, with rucksack and heavy shoes, is rapidly becoming extinct. Box Hill station is not much changed, either, except that it is now Box Hill and Westhumble. But the quiet country road is now a roaring motor-road with an endless stream of cars, and the country pub is a smart hotel. Epsom, too, is no longer a quiet little country town, but an extension of suburbia, and the downs are no longer such very nice walking, being too readily accessible for cars.

But Leith Hill has still a wild lonely splendour of heather, bracken and pine trees, and if you go up from Coldharbour—

having walked from Holmwood station and crossed a stile and an uphill field, up into beech-woods, carpeted in May with bluebells, and down the other side, and bear away over to the right, you may walk for hours and meet no one at all. If you keep on long enough, and cross a motor-road and some fields and the railway line, you may climb up through woods to the old coaching road that runs out over Ranmore Common and drops down to Dorking. It takes about five hours from Holmwood station, but the views are tremendous, and it is, as my father would have said, very nice walking—in spring when the larches are green, in summer when the heather is purple, in the autumn when the beech woods are a glory. And in winter, after a fall of snow, it all looks like Switzerland.

From Guildford you can get a 'bus to Ewhurst and go up Pitch Hill, which also is wild and splendid and free of motorists; and if you are a motorist you can go to Godalming and drive out to some woods, Haydon's Ball, and park your car in the indicated place, then climb up through the woods to the viewpoint at the summit of the hill; it is not as fine a view as from Leith Hill, lacking the great sweep, but on a clear day, I am told, you can see the sea. There is still good walking in the Surrey hills because, fortunately, there are still places inaccessible to cars. I write as one who does not own a car, and who in general dislikes and deplores them, but I am well aware that there are still people who, although they own cars, rejoice in the fact that there are still places accessible only on foot.

One Surrey hill there is which it is convenient to ascend by car, or by 'bus from Guildford Station; that is Stag's Hill, surmounted by Guildford's Cathedral of the Holy Spirit, consecrated in its almost complete stage in May, 1961. The foundation stone was laid in 1939, but the work was held up by the war and not resumed until as late as 1952.

It is a red brick Gothic structure highly reminiscent of the great cathedral of Albi, in south-west France, near Toulouse, though I have nowhere seen Albi acknowledged as the source of its inspiration. The architect of the cathedral, Sir Edward Maufe, describes[1] the plan of its construction as a true cross and a 'symbol of the way of the Faithful being led forward by the rhythm of the arches on each side toward the altar—irresistibly forward without any interruption of screens or pulpitum—something new and very different from cathedrals created from a monastic tradition'. He acknowledges, with satisfaction, that Guildford has been called 'the most functional of all our cathedrals'.

It has also been said of it that, along with the new Anglican cathedral at Liverpool, it is the 'final fling of the Gothic revival'. Within those terms of reference it is undoubtedly architecturally very fine, with a tremendous loftiness and sweep—what the architect calls 'reaching up to enclose great spaces to inspire worship'. This is imaginative, and the fact that only traditional materials have been used in its construction: the interior is of a beautiful light cream sandstone from Somerset, the stone for the exposed parts of windows and copings is a sturdy lime-stone from Rutland; even the bricks were made from the clay of the hill on which the cathedral stands; the chancel and sanctuary are paved with Purbeck freestone. The stag is a kind of *leit-motif*, worked into the needlework of kneelers, into the carpet in front of the high altar, into the bishop's mitre, and elsewhere, including a brass stag in the floor. All is light and bright, with wonderful views from all sides, and there are Eric Gill stone carvings, and glass doors engraved with angels, reminiscent of Coventry.

Having said that it is architecturally very fine I do not find much more to say about it, because for me it is totally lacking in religous atmosphere. I could not find that it had anything to do with the Founder of the Christian religion. The most moving thing there is a rather beautiful statue of St. Francis and

1. In *Guildford Cathedral*, Pitkin Pride of Britain Books, 1966.

the birds, and the most interesting a contemporary wood-carving of the Madonna and Child in the Lady Chapel. Outside, at the top of the tower, a golden angel with outstretched arm serves as a weather vane.

On the south side of the exterior, under the windows, are statues representing the Seven Christian Virtues, among which it is surprising—anyhow, to me—to find prudence. Who decreed, I found myself wondering, that 'discretion, worldly-wisdom, sagaciousness', should be regarded as a virtue? And temperance? Jesus at Cana, at the marriage feast, turned the water into wine, and there was wine at the Last Supper. Courage, one of the seven virtues, is depicted as a knight in armour; Hope is somewhat obscurely represented by St. Christopher and the Christ Child.

Entrance through an oak revolving door seems somehow wrong, more suited to entry into a bank or hotel than into a church; it is a small and awkward revolving door, too, causing one to fumble and stumble a way in and out.

The hilltop position is very fine, but it is some way out of the town, and marching round the exterior in the cold wind I agreed with the woman who remarked to her companion that it seemed to her all 'too remote'. My own companion, my librarian friend, Mr. Gilbert Turner, said, apropos of this overheard observation, that he had been there once when evensong was going on and had noticed that there were about only half a dozen people present—and the seating capacity of the cathedral is 1750. We agreed that a cathedral should be in the city, part of the life of the community, so that people can pop in at any time to say a prayer, or merely to sit quietly, or even, as in Vienna, to take a short cut through.

It is significant that when we drove back down the hill we did not talk about the cathedral; there was nothing to say. We had inspected a distinguished piece of modern Gothic. No spiritual or emotional impact had been made.

On the slopes below the cathedral the foundations of Surrey

University are being laid, and my thoughts went back to Cedar House and Clapham Common. The students will miss the convenience of the 'buses passing the door when they are marooned out there on Stag's Hill in a few years' time. For them, too, the splendid situation is likely to prove 'too remote'.

5

The White Cliffs

In the late 'twenties and early 'thirties, when my generation were young and gay, and the jackboots hadn't begun marching about Europe, it was fashionable to deride England as all that was hypocritical, humbugging and boring, and to skip across to the Continent on every possible occasion, for a life allegedly richer and fuller, freer and more amusing. The best view of the white cliffs of Dover, we liked to declare, caustically, was as they receded on the Channel crossing to Calais. The further off from England the nearer is to France, as it says in *Alice*, and the good life, as we conceived it, was, of course, based on the Left Bank of Paris. Air-travel was not as common then as it is now, and we crossed by sea for the most part; it was cheaper, and we had the pleasure of seeing the white cliffs, the symbol of all we detested, receding.

I tramped the low and uninteresting cliffs behind Dieppe some thirty years and more before I set foot on the high white cliffs of Dover. Though, to be sure, I knew as a child the high and beautiful cliffs behind Hastings, with the ruins of William the Conqueror's castle, for we spent our annual holidays there; and down through the years I have on occasion walked from Eastbourne over Beachy Head and the Seven Sisters and down to Seaford, which is a very fine cliff walk, and once with my daughter I went on from there, up over the Newhaven Heights

and on through Peacehaven and Rottingdean to Brighton, and
that is a very considerable walk, not so much for the mileage as
because it involves a good many cliff-top ups and downs. But
until I came to write this book Dover had no existence except
as a port for the Continent. This I now freely acknowledge was
a very great pity.

For Dover is a pleasant and interesting old town, and its
Norman castle, crowning the white cliffs, is in a fine state of
preservation. It was pleasant, too, I found, to make the journey
by a train that was not a crowded boat-train—it was, in fact, if
anything a racegoers' train, most of the passengers getting off at
a halt near Folkestone for the race-course visible from the train
window, at which there was a meeting that day. It was a grey,
sea-misty April day when I made the journey, the sea as grey as
the mist and almost invisible, but there was the old familiar
Kentish scene of hop-fields and oast-houses and orchards, and
there were tiny lambs keeping close to their ewes in half-
flooded fields. Then there was Folkestone, grey houses crowded
in its cleft between the cliffs, with the harbour beyond, and the
pale glimmer of the sea, and soon after that not the Dover
Station of one's youth with the steamer excitingly waiting,
getting up steam, beyond the Customs' sheds, but the
small quiet station of Dover Priory, and the sea nowhere
in sight.

But as soon as you leave the station you hear and see gulls,
and there is the smell of the sea, and being uncertain which
direction to take I followed some young lads carrying heavy
rucksacks, and in their wake came quickly to the main street, at
the end of which an ornate and noble-looking building caught
my attention. Having done my homework before I set out I
guessed this to be the Maison Dieu, founded in the thirteenth
century by Hubert de Burgh, the royal Constable, 'for the reception of pilgrims of all nations'. In the time of Henry VIII it
became the crown victualling office, which it remained until as
late as 1830, when it became the town hall, though a new town

hall, adjoining the old one, was opened three years later. In 1949 part of this was opened as a museum to replace the war-damaged one in Market Square, and this museum is still there. In 1949, also, the very beautiful seventeenth-century house known as Maison Dieu House, round the corner from the Maison Dieu itself, was restored for use as a public library, which it became in 1952. In the seventeenth century it was the residence of the agent victualler. In 1904 it was purchased by the corporation and used as offices until 1949. I thought it one of the most beautiful houses I had ever seen, in its dignity and graciousness and the symmetry of its proportions.

I continued on along Maison Dieu Road, signposted for the National Monument of Dover Castle. There were also sign-posts for the docks, with *quai* in brackets. I thought that outside of Ireland I had never seen so many pubs; they seemed to recur every few yards, and it makes Dover seem a very friendly place. Somewhere along the Maison Dieu Road I asked a school-girl of fifteen or sixteen if she could direct me to the nearest way up to the castle. It loomed above me, but the road seemed to go on and on, and I needed a way up. The girl asked me whether I wanted the easy way, which, she said, was longer, or the hard way which was shorter. I said I always preferred the short-and-sharp.

She began to direct me and then abruptly stopped. 'Come on,' she said, 'I'll show you.' So we walked along together, she politely crossing to the outside of the pavement—'I feel uncomfortable walking on the inside,' she said, covering this gallantry with the self-consciousness of the young. I told her I hadn't been in Dover before, except to make the Channel crossing, when I was young, and now I had come specially to see the castle. She asked me where I came from and I said Lon-don. She asked what part, and I said Wimbledon. She said that was a nice part, and she herself came from Acton. 'Would you like still to be living there?' I asked. '*Would* I?' she cried. I asked, in some surprise, for I had expected a quite different answer, 'You don't like living in Dover?' She replied, vehemently, 'It's *desperate*!' I urged that surely in the summer it was nice? She conceded that it was better in the summer, a bit more life, but nobody stayed in Dover; they only went through it on the way to somewhere else. 'Don't you get French people over in the summer?' I asked. 'Oh yes, they come,' she said, wearily, 'but the French boys have nothing on the English boys!' Feeling there was no useful comment I could make on that sweeping assertion I changed the subject and asked if there was a 'bus to Deal, as, I said, I thought I would like to go there before leaving the area. She told me where to get the 'bus, and added, 'There's a lot more life to Deal than there is here!'

The short-and-sharp way up to the castle proved to be up a passage way of steps called Harold's Passage, leading out into terraced woodland, where the tree-tops were full of rooks' nests. Almost immediately we came to some iron gates, beyond which some modern buildings were visible, and a board announced that this was a Secondary School for Girls. 'Your school?' I inquired. 'That's it,' the girl replied, resignedly. I thanked her for showing me the way, and she said it was all right . . .

I toiled on up through the woods; it was steep, and when I paused for breath an elderly woman coming down smiled at me. 'Look at the way you've still got to go!' she said, amiably sadistic.

'I'll make it, or die in the attempt,' I assured her.

'Oh, don't say that!' she cried, laughing merrily, and teetered on down the hill.

I continued on up, stopping every few yards, and thinking about the young girl, and wondering what she could find to do in Acton in the summer that she couldn't do better in Dover, with the beaches and the sea, and all those wide-open spaces of the cliff-tops. Maybe in Dover the coffee-bars were fewer and not as good; maybe the boys were duller; maybe Dover isn't as 'swinging' . . . though down in the high street I had observed that the skirts seemed quite as 'mini' as in London.

I came out at last on to the motor-road to Deal, and across it there was, as the young girl had said, a road closed to traffic, 'but you can go up it', so I went up, under the massive walls of the castle. It was closed to traffic, I found, because part of it had collapsed.

According to one authority the summit of Castle Hill, which is over 300 feet above sea-level, has been a continuously fortified site for at least 2000 years, 'for there is evidence of earthwork pre-dating the Roman castrum'. There are the remains of a Roman pharos up there, close beside St. Mary's fortress church, which is of Saxon origin. The church was locked, and the inside of the massive tower of the pharos full of ladders and scaffolding. The official guide suggests that the church was probably built during the reign of Canute, in the eleventh century, and that additional windows were added in the thirteenth. It seems that 'in modern times the church was long roofless and deserted. It was repaired and consecrated about the middle of the last century, at which date the unhappy internal decoration was carried out.' It is suggested that the church was designed in relation to the pharos, which was intended to serve as a west tower. The pharos is castellated and does not look like a lighthouse, but it was identified as such not only because of its situation on the hill top, 'which would render any other explanation difficult', but because it resembles a Roman lighthouse as illustrated 'by the classical texts and numerous representations'. The guide book adds that 'the absence of re-used material in the Dover structure is in favour of a date early in the Roman occupation'.

Having failed to get into the church, and having peered into the pharos and looked up it, and walked all round it, I retraced my steps to the great square keep, with its rectangular towers and curtain wall, all of which are twelfth century. The castle area is entered through Canon's Gate, at the end of the small

Canon's Gate Road under the outer wall; you cross a draw-bridge and are then inside the precincts and can either follow a road along to the keep or branch off to the church and pharos. There are various stone-built houses, which include a restaurant (snack-bar), a bookshop, for guides and postcards, a picnic room, and the houses of various officials. There is also a stables, complete with horses. You can wander freely about here and inspect the various towers—one of which is called Godsfoe —but there is a small charge—1s. 6d.—for admission to the keep. With the towers and drawbridges and inner and outer walls it is all a little like Carcassonne, even to the wide views out over the surrounding countryside. The interior of the keep is full of armour displayed in vast bare halls, and there are numerous stone spiral staircases leading to a labyrinth of galleries and up to the roof; the spiral staircases and galleries are a little eerie, but they are well signposted and there is no danger of getting lost. The small rooms opening off from the great halls and from the galleries are badly lacking in signs indicating what they were used for, and the guide book does not offer much in the way of clues. One was obviously a chapel; others could have served as storerooms. In a lower room there is a huge model of the Battle of Waterloo in a glass case, with a magnifying glass through which to gaze at it. It shows the disposition of the troops, and looked at through the magni-fying glass is astonishingly realistic. The Captain William Siborne, who made it, was a surveyor and historian of the 1815 campaign. He made an accurate on-the-spot survey of the battlefield and completed the work in 1838. He made two models, of which this is the smaller. The original is in the National Army Museum at Camberley; this one became the property of the Tower of London Armouries, who transferred it to Dover in 1963.

Harold built a fortress on the hill, on the higher ground occupied by the church and lighthouse, but only an outline of the southern part can still be traced. This fortress was built in accordance with the promise made to William of Normandy by Harold in 1064. He undertook to build a castle and the essential well—since a fortress cannot withstand a siege without a water supply. Harold made this promise under duress, having been shipwrecked off the French coast and captured by the Normans. He was released only after a sacred oath to support Duke William in his claims to the throne of England.

Harold became king in January, 1066, and died in the Battle of Hastings in October of that year, as we all learned at school. Though we did not learn that he first built a castle for the man who was to be known as William the Conqueror. Nor that his five children, three sons and two daughters, were not by his wife but by his mistress, Ealdgyth (Edith) of the Swan Neck.

The castle, during its long history, was sometimes a royal residence, but it is interesting that Edward III preferred to live in the town in the Maison Dieu. In the course of centuries the castle became increasingly a fortress occupied only by the military, the medieval buildings demolished or adapted to the requirements of successive garrisons.

Before making the descent to the town, down the steep steps of Harold's Passage, I entered the refreshment room, which has been made out of an ancient tower and equipped with strip lighting and a snack-bar. We English, of course, never expect very much of our snack-bars and refreshment rooms, particularly at national monuments, but I wondered about the French family at a nearby table, though they seemed cheerful enough; perhaps for them our unexciting refreshments are all part of our amusing foreignness. I noticed, however, that they were not risking our coffee, nor even our national beverage, a nice-cup-of-tea, but were making merry with Coca-Cola . . .

The 'bus ride along the coast from Dover to Deal takes about half an hour and the road goes through St. Margaret's, with lanes leading out across the cliff-tops and down to the bay. St. Margaret-at-Cliffe, I noticed, was the correct name, and this seemed right and proper. There were cottage gardens gay with mauve and purple aubretia, and the last daffodils and the first tulips, and women got on and off with shopping baskets and greeted each other, neighbourly, in the country manner. They wore rather long tweed coats and decent-looking velour hats.

Walmer flows imperceptibly into Deal, and the sea comes closer. Deal Castle is at the side of the road; it is low and squat, with six fat round towers encircling six inner towers and the circular central tower. Between the inner and outer towers there is a moat. According to the handout of Deal Corporation's Publicity Department, 'When Henry VIII ringed England's southern coast with a mighty network of coastal defences, Deal was chosen as the site for the largest castle of this system . . . During the Civil War, local Parliamentary supporters occupied the castle, only to be driven from it by the Royalist fleet in the Downs; the arrival of a highly trained Parliamentary army, however, led to its recapture. In the eighteenth century, residential quarters were added to this purely defensive fortress, but most of the addition was destroyed by enemy action in 1940, and the rest has now been cleared, revealing the symmetry of the sixteenth-century structure.'

I regarded it with interest from the 'bus window, but the grey elderly woman at my side assured me there was nothing in it, nothing to see, she said. There was more at Walmer Castle.

I was sorry about that, but I couldn't go back. Walmer Castle is anyhow more in the nature of a stately home, with gardens open to the public independently of the castle (castle and gardens 1s. 6d., gardens only, 3d.). It is the official residence of the Lords Warden of the Cinque Ports. Two famous Lords Warden were William Pitt the Younger, and the first Duke of Wellington, who died there, in 1852. Some of the rooms are furnished as in their time. Sir Winston Churchill was a recent Lord Warden.

The 'bus reached a point on the sea-front where, said my companion, 'we all get off'. I got off and looked about. There were fishing boats drawn up on the ridge of shingly beaches, there was a pier going out far into the sea, there were beds of tulips, and pleasant Georgian houses, and narrow side streets. The houses in these side streets, I saw as I walked along, were much older, relics of the days when Deal was a busy seaport of fishermen, smugglers, and the merchants who made a living out of victualling the ships, both merchantmen and men-of-war, which put into the Downs, the tricky stretch of water between the mainland and the dangerous Goodwin Sands. Because of the Goodwins the services of pilots and lifeboat men were much in demand in those days of sail—and still are today. The boatmen of seventeenth-century Deal were known as 'hovellers', and were apparently both derided and admired for their daring. From the time of Elizabeth I until as late as 1864 a navy yard was maintained in Deal for the supply of equipment and stores to warships. When it was demolished in 1864 a new town was built on the site and Deal began its career as a seaside holiday resort. Its lifeboat service is still active and famous, and Deal still serves shipping held up in the difficult roadstead of the Downs. The parish church of St. Leonard, in Upper Deal, the old part of the town, dates from the thirteenth century, and there are some Roman remains, but it was rebuilt in 1604.

The white cliffs end at Deal—the town is recorded in the Domesday Book as *Ad Delam*, 'a low open plain upon the seashore'. The Saxon word for plain is *Dylle*. A plaque along the shore, put up in 1946 and unveiled by the mayor, commemorates the 2000th anniversary of the landing of Julius Caesar, on August 25, 55 B.C., 'on Deal foreshore'. The Roman galleys did not, in fact, lay off Deal for the invasion, but off Kingsdown, south of Walmer, but Walmer is part of the borough. From Walmer the Roman legions marched inland to St. Albans and the great civilising mission was on.

I liked Deal very much, but I left it wondering why the

teenager from Acton found 'more life to it' than in busy,
bustling Dover, with its harbour and the coming and going of
ships, with their passengers and crews. Not to mention all those
French boys, even though they may have nothing on the
English. . . .

6

Vintage Villages of the South Midlands

A FRIEND to whom I had written that for the purposes of this book I intended exploring some of the obscure villages in Central England wrote back that he didn't know there were any, and that it sounded like Livingstone and Central Africa, and he hoped the natives would prove friendly. . . .

Everybody, I suppose, who knows anything about England has at least heard of such famous places as Broadway, Chipping Norton, Northleach, Burford; but who knows anything about the ancient villages of Aynho and King's Sutton on the Northamptonshire-Oxford border? And Bloxham, and Adderbury, and Long Crendon, and Ewelme? Yet these small, remote villages are some of the most beautiful in Central England—perhaps in the whole country, since it is difficult to imagine any more beautiful, and they are beautiful in their own right, by virtue of their architectural simplicity and the good honest regional stone of which they are built, not dolled-up with carriage lamps and blue paint and olde-worlde effects.

This does not mean, however, that they are occupied exclusively, or even mainly, by the natives. Sometimes it means that a village has been taken over by the National Trust, which in some instances cannot afford to let cottages cheaply to the local people but must find tenants who can afford to pay for the necessary modernisation themselves. This can create a housing problem for the present generation of villagers. The Trust frankly admits the problem exists, but can see no way out. It was quoted in *The Times*, November 1, 1966, in a report on the Wiltshire village of Lacock, as saying, 'We cannot let the cottages as they are because there would be attacks on us as slum landlords. We have to, and we want to, modernise. We cannot afford to do it all, so they can only go to people who can pay. We are concerned to keep a village community, and its character. It is our job to preserve this. With our finances, though, it is unavoidable that some properties will go to more wealthy people.'

In the case of Lacock it has been suggested that one way out may be for the Trust to get a Ministry of Housing grant through the Historic Buildings Council for the repair of the village. But in general the problem remains, and it lets in the sophisticated outsiders from London and the north, the retired army majors, doctors, bank managers, who at least preserve the physical character of the villages, whilst the 'natives' move away to the towns, or to the new council housing estates outside the village—where the ceilings are higher, the rooms lighter, and the kitchens much more convenient; so all is not lost. The National Trust problems apart, there is anyhow a tendency for the local people to move out when these old houses fall into disrepair; to rethatch a roof can be too big a problem in modern times—difficult to find anyone to do the job, and expensive, and anyhow is it worth it for the sake of going on living among the decaying old oak beams? Then a middle-class lady from London, perhaps, buys the dilapidated old place cheaply and spends a good deal on its restoration, and in this way the ancient English villages are preserved, even without the services of the National Trust.

These 'protected' English villages are not confined to the Oxford-Northants-Bucks borders, but with the ever-increasing area of commuter country they have become in the last few years almost non-existent in the Home Counties. Suburbia can now spread a very long way out, even into 'beechy Bucks'—Chalfont St. Peter is a case in point, a place, now, of 'homes of quality', car-parks, and bulldozers scooping up slabs of fields in the process of converting a lovely country road into a great motor-road.

Chalfont St. Giles, a little further on, is the village in which Milton lived for a time to escape the Great Plague; the cottage was acquired for the nation in 1887; it is still there and open to visitors. There is a certain amount of suburban building at each side of the motor-road, but the village itself is tucked away in a wooded hollow, off the road. Only a mile and a half from Gerrards Cross, however, it is now well within the commuter belt, with shops invading the village green.

It is many years since I was in Buckinghamshire and it was pleasant to see again the gently undulating farm lands, both pasture and corn lands, crowned, as I had remembered them, with the characteristic clumps of beech woods.

The approach to Amersham gives no hint of joys to come. A gasometer looms up, there are suburban houses, with aubretia massed mauve and purple on the stone walls of chronically well-kept gardens, and at the side of the road as it swings round there is a large modern factory for the production of sausages and meat-pies—the ultimate end to which the pigs reared in the district must come. But Gilbert Turner, who had undertaken to drive me to these lesser-known villages of the South Midlands, assures me that all this modern development has been kept well away from the famous old town itself. Lying back from the road, crowning a low hill above fields and park land, is a beautiful old yellow house called Shardeloes, a stately home now converted into expensive apartments. It was taken over from the original architect by Robert Adam, whose 'imprint' is left in the form of the characteristic portico. Great areas of the countryside here are being swallowed up by road-widening—there is no escaping the times.

But Amersham High Street is so beautiful that it should be

preserved as a National Monument, for at both sides are half-timbered sixteenth- and seventeenth-century houses and inns, and handsome red brick Georgian houses, and in the middle there is a red brick town hall with a square tower, seventeenth century and very attractive, and there are lovely almshouses of the same period. I was very excited by Amersham High Street; I wanted to get out of the car and inspect it more closely, but Gilbert, whilst agreeing that it was very fine, drove firmly on; Amersham was to be found in any guide-book or encyclopedia; our objective was lesser-known England . . .

So we drove on through Little Missenden, a nice small village lying beside the road, and on to Great Missenden, a pleasant old town, not as insistently picturesque as Amersham, but a 'real' place, not art-and-crafty, with red brick and flint houses . . . and a block of modern flats; and outside a road going off in the direction of a wooded hill, signposted to The Hale.

Then Wendover, with trees in the streets and Georgian houses, and older houses, and blossoming pear trees topping old walls, but degenerating outside into a dreary nothingness.

Towards Aylesbury the countryside flattens out, and the houses we come to are ugly. When I remark on the general pervading dreariness Gilbert says, briefly, 'This is Puritan country. No teas served on Sundays!' as though that accounts for everything. In the town there are tall modern blocks, and one monstrous skyscraper tower. There is a red brick County Hall and more modern blocks at the town centre. There is also a Victorian clock monument and a statue of John Hampden. but there is a twelfth- to thirteenth-century church, and seventeenth- to eighteenth-century houses in the streets of the older part of the town converging on to the market square. Many years ago I was in Aylesbury visiting the girls' Borstal institution, when Lilian Barker was governor, but I had no recollection of the town from that time. The outskirts of the town are Victorian and hideous, the roof-tops a forest of television aerials. There is an industrial zone, and some well-designed modern housing estates.

The general drear continues on to Bicester, with what I begin to think of as the inevitable road construction. Beyond the havoc of the bulldozed countryside, however, there is a kind of oasis in the wilderness in the shape of the pleasant country road which leads on to Waddesdon, famous for its manor, the great house built for the Rothschilds and now owned by the National Trust. It contains, apparently, among other treasures, a great wealth of French porcelains and tapestries. Five arrows is the crest of the Rothschild family, and near the entrance to the manor is the Five Arrows Hotel.

By the dusty side of the road a party of people, their car drawn into the verge, picnic with brightly coloured tables and striped garden chairs with tubular steel arms. Behind the hawthorn hedges there are woods and fields, fresh and shining in their spring green, but they prefer the dusty verge, with the cars whizzing past. People are curious.

We are now in the Midlands Plain of north Bucks, but it is not all that flat, and there are stands of trees, and fields full of black and white cows—innumerable cows. But after Waddesdon there is a dull straight road of the kind that could go on forever, and pylons march relentlessly across the landscape. The flatness and dullness of this part of Oxfordshire is in marked contrast with the Cotswold area to the west.

Bicester, too, when you reach it, is a dull little town, redeemed to some extent by some old stone houses and some good modern school buildings. The vast army ordnance depot dominates all else; it stretches away on both sides of the main road, with its conglomeration of barbed wire and army huts. Gilbert says he knew a young man who did his military service there, in the days of conscription, and he hated it so much that now, when driving in the area, he makes enormous détours to avoid passing through Bicester.

Soon after unloved and unlovely Bicester we come to Aynho just over the border in Northants, and this must surely be one of the most beautiful villages in England. There is some 'development' just outside, in the shape of a colony of council houses, but they are built of stone, and are of good design. The village itself consists entirely of sixteenth- and seventeenth-century houses, built of stone, and many of them with apricot trees trained cordon fashion across their fronts. There is the village centre, called the Square, where there is an inn, a combined stores and post-office, a butcher's shop, and a small general stores where you can get tea. The road then dips down, with a fine panorama of open country ahead, and narrow lanes opening off to the right, with interesting names, such as Skittle Alley, and Hollow Way, with stone-built cottages with gardens full of flowers in front, and a silence which is almost too intense, for not only are there no sounds of cars or 'planes, but not even the crow of a cock, the bark of a dog, or any human sound. Only a scent of wallflowers and the deep stillness. I remembered the Irishman in Connemara years ago; he was delivering a load of turf to my cottage and he remarked on the silence. 'It's too quiet here,' he declared. 'Too quiet be far!' He longed for the day when he would be able to get back to London, to Hammersmith Broadway, and its splendid roar and clatter.

I cried to Gilbert in a kind of anguish, 'It's so beautiful, but what would you do if you lived here?'

He seemed surprised.

'Presumably you would do as you do in London—write and read.'

'But when I wasn't writing or reading,' I persisted, 'what would one do then, in a place like this?'

'Well, I don't know—work in the garden, I suppose . . .'

'I would never see my friends!' I cried. 'They'd never come so far, and I wouldn't be able to afford to keep going into London to see them. And I would never go to a cinema or a theatre or an art exhibition. And no bookshops. And the nearest town—Bicester!'

'Or Banbury,' he suggested.

When we got back to the Square I noticed a 'bus stop.

'Ah,' I cried, in relief, 'a 'bus stop! They can get out!'

We got back into the car and inside ten minutes were in a village almost as beautiful, King's Sutton. There is a very fine Tudor manor house there, with mullioned windows, and a fifteenth-century church in which there is a big old stone font said to be 900 years old, at which St. Rumbold was christened, he having demanded this as soon as he was born. . . .

But whereas Aynho was almost perfect, at King's Sutton a garishly blue-painted co-operative stores spoils the grey stone scene round the church. The church has a noble spire, and some interesting gargoyles. Away from the grassy village centre, by the church, there are council houses, but, as elsewhere in this area, stone-built and of good design.

There were intimations of life in this village. A county-looking lady in a hacking jacket, her breeches tucked into wellingtons, charged about on the grassy triangle in front of her handsome half-timbered house in the wake of a motor mower; and two little girls were stretched out face downwards on the churchyard wall reading, or playing at reading, their books. A small white poodle scampered over the grass, and a black cat sat on the wall of a cottage garden.

We drove on through dreary Oxfordshire something-and-nothing country to Banbury, the outskirts of which are suburban with 'ribbon development', but which is itself a genial prosperous town, with golden-coloured stone buildings, and an ugly Georgian church, and, of course, Banbury Cross of the nursery rhyme, though the original was destroyed by the Puritans in 1602, and the present Victorian monument was erected on the site in 1859 and added to in 1914. It has Queen Victoria at one side of it and King Edward VII at the other, and is not a thing of beauty. But Banbury is an attractive, busy town, with an air of market-town prosperity. There is a pleasant high street, with flower-baskets suspended from the lamp standards, and gay with daffodils—real ones—the day we drove through. The earth in this area is as red as in Devon, with fields churned up by open-cast iron-ore mining. The mounds of earth are left and in time the grass grows over, and strangely shaped hillocks and mounds are left which do not enhance the dull landscape.

But soon there is Wroxton, with thatched houses of yellow stone, and a big old house lying back across its park, Wroxton College, of the Farleigh Dickinson University. Nearby is a lovely house with stone-framed windows, called Mullions, which calls for some exclamation from me because I called a house in my novel, *Proud Heaven*,[1] by that name and believed I had invented a rather clever name for a house with mullioned windows. My Mullions was a Tudor manor house in Worcestershire—'the very heart of England'. In the Norwegian translation the title was changed to *England's Hjerte*, England's Heart. (But the French translation, published in Brussels, would have none of that, and called it simply, *Double Concerto*, because Bach's Concerto for Two Violins was its *leit-motif*.)

Some of the thatched houses in Wroxton have fallen into disrepair, their roofs collapsing, sadly. Gilbert and I reflect that if we had the money we could each buy one and do it up and sell it and make a lot of money . . . if we had the money. It is desperately quiet here, except for some muted pop music from a transistor at the feet of a group of three boys and a girl leaning against the railing of a duck pond. They are all about fifteen and they all wear jeans. The girl has a bicycle on which she wiggles about; suddenly she seems to have had enough of the boys' banter and rides off; the boys go on leaning. I find myself speculating on what else there is for them to do in a place like this on a mildly pleasant Saturday afternoon in early spring. When you have been born and bred in a place there is no point tramping across the dull flat fields, or up and down the lanes, to

1. 1944.

nowhere in particular. You could stay indoors and read, but it is in the nature of youth to get out of the house. For the adults of the modern English village there are plenty of activities, through the Women's Institutes, the Young Farmers' Clubs, bingo sessions, and the social life that adults manage to make for themselves anywhere, in and out of each others' homes, and for the men the pubs, and for the women their domestic interests, but for the young ones, the boys and girls, the *kids* . . . what is there for them? Observing that group that afternoon I did just wonder.

We drive through sleepy Wroxton and turn into a side road; there are no cars and no people; only the green countryside, gently undulating, flowing away on both sides, and a sense of there being, after all, wide areas of England still left 'undeveloped'. Edge Hill was a low ridge in the near distance. The Battle of Edgehill, vaguely one remembers what one learned at school; nobody won, did they? Neither the King nor Parliament? Anyhow, it all happened over there, on the Warwickshire border. I reflect that sometime I must re-read *1066 and All That* and brush up my English history. . . .

We are at the edge of the great Midland Plains, and soon we come to Bloxham, which, after a suburban approach, is revealed as a pleasant village of stone houses and cottages, with a handsome church with an impressive spire, with pinnacles, and a huge Gothic-revival building we later discovered to be Bloxham School, a minor public school. We get out of the car to inspect the church and are half-deafened by a tremendous crash of bells. From the number of cars outside the churchyard we think perhaps a wedding is in progress, but we march boldly in—only to discover that the church is empty and the commotion is bell-practice. We learn from a leaflet in the church that there is a peal of eight bells, and that the tenor bell was cast in 1648 and is the largest in Oxfordshire, outside Christ Church Cathedral. The church is St. Mary's, but the leaflet refers to it as the church of Our Ladye of Blokesham

F

Through the Centuries. It dates from the twelfth century; the tower and spire were built in the fourteenth. There are several features of interest in the church. One is an almost obliterated medieval mural of St. Christopher over the north door; another is a chancel east window by William Morris and Burne-Jones, which I regarded respectfully without liking it very much, though I have an immense respect and admiration for William Morris as an authentic socialist, and a considerable craftsman and poet.

We drive the short distance on to Adderbury, and there is again the 'development' approach, but the village is sizable, spreading, with golden stone houses and cottages set among trees, many pubs—always a good sign, the sign of a 'real' place, in which the 'natives' abound—and a handsome spired parish church, the church of St. Mary the Virgin, which John Betjeman[1] has described as 'magnificent', and its exterior 'about the finest in the country'. Bell-practice was in progress here, too, causing a commotion among the rooks in the tree tops and tower. There is a fine east window, with stone traceries, and good stone carvings at the sides. I liked, too, some interestingly realistic carvings of women's heads at the top of two fifteenth-century columns in the north transept. Outside I liked some amusing gargoyles. There is a medieval barn and two very beautiful seventeenth-century houses at one time used by religous orders, but becoming later the Grange, and the Manor House. There is a stream called the Sor brook, by which we walked, and a Gothic-revival school and school-house. I liked Adderbury, and the natives were definitely friendly. . . .

We drove on, over the Oxfordshire border, to Long Crendon, two miles north of Thame. It consists of a very long high street, in which most of the houses are thatched, and more than fifty of which are of the sixteenth and seventeenth century. We tramped the entire length of the high street to a very cold church which contained, nevertheless, a good deal of Early

1. In *English Parish Churches*, 1958.

English work, not often found, and this, too, was called the church of St. Mary the Virgin. There is an extremely beautiful sixteenth-century manor house, and close to the church a fourteenth-century courthouse, a long low two-storey house of red brick and timber, with a red-tiled roof. The huge key is left in the front door and the house is open to inspection. Inside, the court room is upstairs, and has a high ceiling, with some massive beams. According to the available leaflet, 'the building was probably first erected as a wool store or staple hall in the days when the neighbouring county of Oxford sent more wool to the looms of East Anglia than any other, save possibly Middlesex. It was known as the Staple Hall until the second half of the nineteenth century. As the hall was a large and substantial building, it became the custom to hold the manorial courts here as early as the days of Henry V (1413–22), to whose Queen, Catherine of France, one of the manors of Long Crendon was assigned in dower. The courts continued to be held here by successive owners of the manors until recent times. In 1900 the National Trust purchased the courthouse for a nominal sum from Lady Kinloss, All Souls College and the Ecclesiastical Commissioners, the respective owners of the three manors. . . . The whole of the courthouse is now rented by the Buckinghamshire County Council. The ground floor is inhabited by the district nurse, while the upper floor, comprising the long hall, left as it has always been, today does service as an Infant Welfare Centre.' It is one of the earliest National Trust acquisitions.

We trudge back down the long high street, where wall-flowers glow from the tops of walls and from their base, and cottage windows peer out under the bushy eyebrows of their thick thatch, and get back into the car and drive on to Great Haseley, in Oxfordshire, which is all thatched stone cottages, with aubretia everywhere, and rather like Long Crendon, only less so, and we come to a small and very beautiful place set among trees in the hollow of low hills. We stop beside a grassy bank and a little blossoming tree. I crawl out under the tree and stand looking tiredly up at a splendid tall red brick building which I judge to be sixteenth century, but which I learn is early fifteenth—'A pre-Tudor school, still in use,' says Gilbert. He adds, sympathetically, 'It's been a long day, I know, but this is something you had to see!' We are at Ewelme

Here, too, the door is open and we walk in to Ewelme Foundation School, founded as a church school in 1437 and now in the late twentieth century incorporated into the State system and still using its original building. I read the notice in the porch, and transcribe it to my notebook: *In this parish of Ewelme on the 3rd July 1437 King Henry VI granted a licence to his cousin, William de la Pole, the first Duke of Suffolk, and Alice, his wife, to found an almshouse and a school at their manor of Ewelme in Oxfordshire.*

On either side of the wooden staircase are specimens of the work of the present generation of Ewelme—drawings, water-colours, pottery, and other hand-crafts. There are also stories and essays, by young children and older children, and the standard of their work is remarkably high. In the long room at the top of the stairs there are school desks and seats, and a high and fine timbered ceiling. There are further specimens of the children's work. It is an odd thought that children have been learning to read and write, to paint and draw and do hand-crafts, in this room for five centuries without a break.

When we leave we pause to admire the beautiful doors of the school, fine examples of fifteenth-century woodwork, and originally the west doors of the church.

We go on up a little hill with an orchard at one side and a well-kept churchyard with rose trees at the other, to the very beautiful fifteenth-century church, and which, like the school, is virtually as the medieval builders left it. I am not equipped adequately to describe the beauty of this church, but I think I was never in one possessed of such grace, expressed in the arches and in the proportions of the light broad windows set in such delicate stone tracery. The St. John's Chapel, adjoining the chancel, is as wide as the chancel itself, and of the same length, and its light beautiful east window contains fragments of medieval glass. The tomb of Alice, Duchess of Suffolk, between the chancel and the chapel, is a very great treasure. It was erected in the church in 1475, shortly after her death, and is entirely of alabaster. It is built in three tiers: on the first lies the figure of the duchess, her hands folded in prayer, and most beautifully modelled, on her head a coronet, and above her head an elaborate canopy carved from a single block of alabaster; purely as a work of art this sculpture of the duchess is a masterpiece. Below this effigy is the tomb chest which contains the remains of the duchess and which, also, is beautifully carved; below this again is a kind of arcade, which contains a gruesome skeletonised effigy of the duchess in death, clothed in a shroud; what is strange is that the roof of this 'arcade' has been painted with frescoes which can only be seen by anyone who lies almost flat on the ground—which I did—and peers in; a little later in the evening they would not have been visible. A copy of the frescoes hangs in a frame at the chancel side of the entrance to the chapel, but it is worth making the effort to see them *in situ*.

In St. John's Chapel, also, is the tomb of Thomas Chaucer, who died in 1434, and his wife Matilda Burghersh, who died two years later. The tomb, which is of marble, is of more interest than beauty, for Thomas was the son of Geoffrey Chaucer, the poet. The only daughter of Thomas and Matilda was Alice, who married as her second husband William de la Pole, then 4th Earl of Suffolk. The tomb of Alice was given by her son, who was born at Ewelme and to whom the manor passed on the death of his father, who was murdered in 1450. This son, John, the 2nd Duke of Suffolk, also gave the remarkable ten-foot-high font cover of carved wood, which consists of four tiers of arches surmounted by a figure of St. Michael.

The wooden roof of St. John's Chapel is very beautifully

carved with angels at the intersections of the beams. The roof had to be restored in 1937 and six of the medieval angels replaced by modern replicas.

From the west door of the church a covered passage way leads to the cloisters, where there is a double door with a notice asking that the privacy of the inhabitants be respected—for the steps lead to the fifteenth-century almshouses, which are still inhabited, just as the fifteenth-century school is still in use. Thirteen little houses are built round a courtyard, and village lads with bicycles were delivering the evening papers. These cloister houses were built by William de la Pole, and his wife Alice, and, says the historical guide, 'No other brick buildings of such an early date are known in this part of England and the style suggests that the workmen came from the Duke's chief Manor of Wingfield in Suffolk ... Almsmen are appointed by the Lord of the Manor, the Earl of Macclesfield, who is a Trustee. Their health is cared for by a resident nurse. Each almsman has two rooms which are equipped with modern water supply and electric light.'

I had been tired when we left Long Crendon and not much inclined for taking in anything else, but I was very glad to have seen Ewelme, with its remarkable group of medieval buildings —church, school, almshouses, still in use as such in the late twentieth century, and all set so sweetly in the hollow of the gentle hills, among the fields with their tall elms, and across from them the apple orchard and cottage gardens. Here it is possible to feel that in spite of all the motor-roads that devour the countryside, and 'development' and uglification, old England still stands its ancient ground, its heart beating strongly and indestructibly down through the centuries.

We drove on to Henley-on-Thames after that, through the village of Stonor, where the same Roman Catholic family have been lords of the manor from the twelfth century, the Stonor family. But here the modern world intrudes, for the present owner, Major the Honourable Robert Sherman Stoner, has been in trouble with some of the villagers, who complain that parachutists of the British Parachute Club, of which the major is an honorary member, drop, mostly on Sundays, on Russells Water Common, with his permission (*The Times*, April 24, 1967). The Common is a favourite picnic spot, but the major says he always warns picnickers when there is going to be any parachuting, and disputes the other complaint that the parachuting is going to attract traffic to the village and could cause jams. My own sympathies are all with the protesting villagers and their parish council; it seems a pity that people who have managed to get away from the Sunday traffic on the roads and settled down for a peaceful picnic on a common, should suddenly have to scramble their sandwiches and thermos flasks together and move off to somewhere else, for fear of invasion from the air.

With that bad mark against the lord of the manor it seems only fair to add that Stonor Park Manor House is readily available to the public, and its Catholic chapel is always open, as it has always been.

These few notes are only an indication of what is to be found in the South Midlands; there are in this area innumerable other beautiful villages with stone-built and half-timbered cottages of the fifteenth, sixteenth, and seventeenth centuries, in good repair and still inhabited, some thanks to the National Trust, others to individual enterprise.

Nor, of course, are all the old villages to be found here; they exist all over England, little known, unsung, largely unvisited, but *lived* in—even though the 'natives' may in some instances have moved out to the new council housing estates just outside; but then a new generation of natives is established. One way or another the precious national heritage is maintained, and it is what the poet Edmund Blunden has called[1] a 'marvellous possession of the sense and spirit'.

1. In *English Villages*, 1942.

7

Coventry: Ancient and Modern

THE journey by train to Coventry took me back, for the first time in years, to Euston Station, to which I went several times a year for the seventeen years I had a cottage in the West of Ireland. For a long time it had been exciting to drive in under the great Victorian archway and board the Irish Mail for Liverpool; in the course of time it began to be increasingly a chore and finally a bore; the long love-affair with the land of my ancestors had come to an end—as all love-affairs must.

The Euston to which I returned was unrecognisable and bewildering; gone was the great yellow archway—the once romantic Gateway to Ireland—and all the other old familiar yellow shabbinesses—and the Irish faces and the Irish voices; perhaps there are still Irish porters at Euston, but I was aware only of coloured porters, a number of women among them, smart in their uniforms. Gone were all the familiar landmarks; the booking-office, the book-stall, the frowsy, friendly place where you got that last cup of tea before the sentimental goodbyes that were always part of being seen-off on the Irish Mail—'My love to Paddy—remember me to Séan. Think of me tomorrow when you see the sun go down on Galway Bay . . .'—Nothing is where it used to be, and instead there is a chaos of reconstruction, and behind a corrugated iron screen a machine is going bom-a-de-bom, bom-a-de-bom, relentlessly;

where areas have been completed, and the rubble and the corrugated iron cleared away, all is white and blue, bright and stream-lined and assertively modern, with efficient-looking bars and cafés, all plate glass and strip lighting and plastic flowers—light and bright and cheerful. How much better than all that old Victorian murk and shabbiness! Well, I suppose so. Seems a pity about the *arch*, though, somehow. It was a part of British railway history, and should surely have been preserved as a national monument. It represented almost a way of life.

Coventry Station, a little over an hour later, is bright and modern, too; but then Coventry was practically rebuilt after 1945, the greater part of the city having been destroyed in the fearful air-raids of 1941, which may be said to have wiped out the very heart of England, for Coventry is, as near as makes no difference, almost in the centre of England, almost equidistant from the four great ports, London, Hull, Liverpool, Bristol.

Coming to a city new to you in your own country can be as exciting as any new foreign city, I discovered; and to a Londoner it is, virtually, that—'belonging to, or proceeding from, other persons and things', and therefore different, and in a sense foreign. Outside the station I boarded a 'bus which said City Centre on the front. It was a pay-as-you-enter 'bus, and as I paid I asked the driver if the new cathedral was at the City Centre, or near it, and before he could answer a woman passenger said eagerly that she was getting off there herself and would show me. She was elderly and kindly, and when we got off showed me where to go down the subway; when I came up on the other side, she explained, I would find the cathedral behind the old parish church—'that's it, over there!' The subway is light and bright and very few people attempt to cross the road. Later I found the handsomely laid out traffic-free shopping centre close by; there is no excuse for getting run-over in rebuilt Coventry.

Before we go any further we had perhaps better get the Lady

Godiva business over-with. We were all, I suppose, brought up on the legend of the beautiful lady who rode naked through the streets of Coventry, her modesty preserved by her long hair, though we were never very clear as to why she did it. Vaguely we believed some evil person had forced her to, from sheer wickedness. The generally accepted version of the story is that the people of Coventry, suffering grievously under the excessive taxation imposed upon them by Leofric, Earl of Mercia and lord of Coventry, his wife, the Lady Godiva, appealed to him on their behalf to lighten their burden. He agreed on condition that she would ride naked through the market-place when all the people were present. She accepted the 'dare' and did so, and Leofric kept his word. 'There is no inherent reason to doubt the story,' says Professor Shaw,[1] 'though its later versions are plainly fictitious.' The Peeping Tom story is a later accretion. 'The earliest account,' says Professor Shaw, 'occurs in the *Flores Historiarum* of Roger of Wendover (died 1237), who borrowed from an unknown earlier writer.' Lady Godiva died in 1085 at the age of forty-five. As the earl died in 1057 Godiva could not have been more than seventeen at the time of her famous ride, and might well have been younger. The bronze equestrian statue of her in the small garden of the City Centre certainly depicts her as a slender girl, seated side-saddle on the horse, her long hair covering one breast and streaming down over her thighs. The words, 'Self-Sacrifice', are engraved on the plinth and below them words attributed to Tennyson, 'Then she rode back clothed on with chastity. She took the tax away and built herself an ever-lasting name.' At the other side of the plinth are the words: 'This statue is dedicated to the city's benefactress of a bygone age and is presented by W. H. Bassett Green to his fellow citizens, 1949.'

Whether the story of the ride is legend or history, Godiva herself, Godgyfu, wife of Leofric, existed; her lands are listed

1. In an article in *Chambers Encyclopedia*, 1959.

in the Domesday survey, and with her husband she founded several monasteries, including the Benedictine monastery which was to be the nucleus of the manor of *Coventreu*, or *Coventre*. The trees and shrubs of the public garden in which her statue stands were a gift from the Dutch people in 1948. Across from the square Leofric is less heroically commemorated by the modern hotel named after him. A 'Godiva procession' was instituted in 1678 as part of Coventry Fair and was kept up, at intervals, until 1826, when it lapsed—perhaps from lack of of candidates for the title role. The statue makes, in my opinion, a very charming centre-piece for the City Centre, though I have been told that there was some objection to it when it was first set up there.

Having admired Lady Godiva in her garden setting, gay at that time with daffodils, I descended and ascended the subway as instructed, and came up on to a pavement flanked by a low grey stone wall, at the top of which, on a sloping flower-bed, some words and a date had been designed in growing plants, but I could not make them out. To the left is the narrow lane of Priory Row, with old timbered houses, and a little beyond them, facing the church, a tall rickety-looking wooden structure with its feet in a wilderness of brambles and long grass; this is Holy Trinity Bell Tower, and the date is given on it as 1864.

A short flight of steps leads up from the pavement to the grassy precincts of Holy Trinity Church, which is fourteenth century, but parts of which date from about 1043, which is proudly announced on a board outside, together with the fact that the citizens of Coventry have been going there to worship since the eleventh century. The church is Perpendicular and its tall spire is one of the three which gave Coventry its name as the City of the Three Spires, the other two being the spire of the old cathedral, nearby, and the ancient spire of Grey Friars Church, which also still stands although the church was destroyed in the raid which destroyed the cathedral and the entire City Centre. The old parish church of the Holy

Trinity, although so close to the cathedral and struck by incendiaries, was miraculously spared, with only minor damage. It is a very beautiful old church with some fine windows in rich deep blues, one of which, the great west window, represents the story of the Church of England; many of the figures in it are copied from old paintings; the lower right panel depicts the Catholic saints, Teresa of Avila and Catherine of Siena. The church has a soaring, grey cathedralesque loftiness, and a gentle grey peacefulness. It should certainly be visited before proceeding to the cathedral.

There were white and purple and yellow crocuses in the little churchyard on the March day I was first there. My attention was caught by an ancient tombstone, which bore the following legend: *Grave of a gladiator, John Parkes, a Native of the City. He was a man of mild disposition, a gladiator by profession, who after having fought 350 battles in the principal parts of Europe with honour and applause, at length quitted the stage and sheathed his sword, and with Christian resignation submitted to the Grand Victor in the 52nd year of his age. Anno 1733.*

It is so pleasant an approach to the cathedral along this short broad walk past the old church that it is a shock to come suddenly upon a garishly painted ice-cream kiosk outside a small café with outdoor tables whose blue sun-umbrellas advertise Pepsi-Cola. . . .

St. Michael's Parish Church, which became the cathedral in 1918, was built at the same time as Holy Trinity. The Provost of Coventry Cathedral, the Very Reverend H. C. N. Williams, in his book,[1] explains the building of the two churches at the same time, and in close proximity to each other, and to the Benedictine priory, as 'witness both to the prodigality of church-building at that time, and to the extent to which status was defended by those who claimed it. Holy Trinity was apparently built for the tenants of the prior's half of the town, and St. Michael's for the tenants of the earl's half of the town.'

1. *Coventry Cathedral*, Pitkin Pride of Britain Books, 1966.

What is exciting, and also moving, is that you come to the new cathedral by way of the old. Suddenly the ruin is there and you find yourself in a wide space open to the sky and enclosed by the shell of a great cathedral. Ahead you see the lofty remains of the great east window; you cross the vast nave, past the stumps of pillars, and come to a small altar behind which there is a cross made of charred wood; in the stone wall at the back of the altar are carved the words: *Father Forgive*. This cross is made from the charred beams which fell from the roof a few days after the bombing; two lengths of the charred but still solid oak were taken and wired together and set up in an old dustbin filled with anti-incendiary bomb sand at the east end of the ruins. This Charred Cross became world-famous, and with the poignancy of the carved words which form the altar's reredos is very moving. In front of the Charred Cross is another precious relic—the Cross of Nails, made from the original fourteenth-century hand-forged nails which fell from the great oak timbers as the roof burned. The morning after that terrible night of the bombing the inspiration came, the Provost tells us, 'to form three of the nails into the shape of a Cross. This Cross has become the symbol of Coventry Cathedral's Ministry of International Reconciliation. Crosses of Nails have been presented to many centres throughout the world where there has been a response to the efforts of the cathedral to establish links of fellowship to study the meaning of Christian Reconciliation in a divided world. . . .' There are Crosses of Nails in various places in Germany, both East and West, in Russia, Norway, Asia, Africa, U.S.A., Canada, Australia.

The Charred Cross, the Cross of Nails, and the words, *Father Forgive*, symbolise the Ministry of Reconciliation to which the cathedral, resurgent from the destruction of war, is dedicated. A small International Centre was established under the sanctuary, in a converted coal cellar and organ-blowing chamber; it was opened in January, 1960, by Dr. Otto Dibelius, Bishop of Berlin, and furnished by an anonymous donor who had lost his entire family in an air-raid on Berlin. In the autumn and winter of 1961-2 a group of young Christians from Germany, calling themselves *Aktion Versöhnung* (Action Reconciliation) gave up their paid employment for six months to come and work at Coventry restoring vestries of the old cathedral as an extension of the International Centre. They were supported by money contributed by individual Christians from all over Germany. In 1965 the John F. Kennedy House, a hostel for young people from all over the world who come to take part in the cathedral's activities, was opened by Herr Willi Brandt, then Mayor of West Berlin. There is Holy Communion before the Charred Cross at 6 a.m. on Easter Sunday, and at 7 a.m. on Whit-Sunday.

A flight of steps leads down directly from the ruins to the huge pillared porch of the new cathedral. This porch is a public thoroughfare, with Priory Street at one end and Cuckoo Lane at the other. Entrance to the cathedral is through glass doors in a huge glass screen, known as the West Screen, engraved with figures of angels and saints, with, also, a Virgin and Child. St. Alban is depicted in the costume of a Roman soldier, which he was before his conversion, but carrying a cross at the end of a long staff. What seems to me very fine about this great screen is that from inside the new cathedral the noble ruins of the old are visible, and that people going about their daily business in the thoroughfare which links new and old can see into the cathedral, so that with all its beauty and wonder it is part of their normal life, not something shut away in a seldom, perhaps never-visited church, intended only for 'religous' people or tourists. The groups of chattering, uniformed school-girls, and the strolling teenagers from the art and technical schools, who pass and re-pass all the time, may not give a glance at what so entrances the visitor, still less think of it all as a 'workshop of God', as the Provost would wish; nevertheless, something of it all is engraved on their sub-conscious minds, as surely as the saints and angels are engraved on the great glass screen. In the best sense, it seems to me, it is *good* for them to have this contact.

What you see when you pass in through the glass screen is a lofty and noble cathedral interpreted in modern terms by fine artists. A tremendous vision is enshrined here. There is a *leit-motif* of the Crown of Thorns. That is as I saw it; the central idea, as expressed in the Charred Cross, and the words, *Father Forgive*, behind, in the sanctuary in the ruins, is Reconciliation. But the Crown of Thorns theme is there too, as I will show. In simple terms, what you see when you enter is a great church full of light and colour, with ten great stained glass windows designed to convey the Destiny of Man at one side of the nave and the Revelation of God at the other. On the pale grey of the walls sayings of Christ are carved in fine uneven lettering on white stone tablets, of which there are eight, and which are called the Tablets of the Word. The unevenness of the lettering is intended to convey the primitive origins of the texts, and the effect is beautiful and moving in its simplicity. Much in this resurgent cathedral I found moving, I who am an unbeliever.

Slender tapering columns support the seventy-foot-high canopy of the ceiling, which has a latticed effect, and is very beautiful. The nave is huge—270 feet long and 80 feet wide. You are in a church capable of holding 2000 people. The tremendous Graham Sutherland tapestry, the largest in the world, taking the place of the traditional east window, and depicting Christ in Glory, with Man between his feet, of course dominates the church. It is a bright green and depicts Christ seated, with upraised hands and wearing a white yoked robe with loose sleeves and a broad sash, such as Christ the Man certainly never wore. But as this depicts Christ in Glory the artist is entitled to his vision. At the bottom of the tapestry is a small panel in grey and black of Christ Crucified. There are also four small panels depicting the four beasts from *Revelations*. The tapestry was woven in France, and took 30,000 hours to make.

I gazed at it respectfully, unable to like it. I have never met anyone who liked it; but that it is impressive is undeniable.

There is a fine, modernistic silver-gilt cross on the high altar, in front of the sombre panel of the Crucifixion, and inset into it a Cross of Nails. Just as the Charred Cross on the altar of the sanctuary in the ruins symbolises Sacrifice, this splendid cross symbolises Resurrection.

Above the stalls at each side of the chancel are 'canopies' like hedges of thorns, forming a 'thorn-like avenue'; this theme is repeated above the bishop's throne near the high altar on the west side of the chancel. They are here surmounted by a bishop's mitre wrought in beaten copper and gilded, and are decorated with nuts and bolts, 'symbolising the industrial interests of the Coventry diocese'. The six candlesticks on the high altar, three at each side, are of pottery; they are 'taller than a man', and believed to be the largest 'thrown' pots in existence. The 'thorn' decorations in part frame the great tapestry. I have heard them likened to hat-racks and complained of; I did not at the time understand their symbolism, but they did not disturb me; in the whole modern context of the cathedral they seemed to me to harmonise, in their warm copper, with the roof, and the rich reds of the fabulous windows.

At the foot of the high altar there is a small Lady Chapel; the lower part of the tapestry, with the Crucifixion, forms the reredos to its altar. A few steps from it is another small chapel, which for me is the most beautiful thing in the cathedral; it is the Chapel of Christ in Gethsemane. The entrance gate is an iron-work grill of a Crown of Thorns, made and given by the Royal Engineers. Through the circle of the crown is seen a most wonderful panel of blue and gold mosaic; at the centre of the panel is Christ holding the Cup of Pain, and to the right, metallic grey on dark blue, are depicted three of the disciples asleep. To the right of the gold mosaic and overlapping the dark part is a simple altar consisting of a narrow stone slab on an upright, with two candles in small simple holders. The artist of this very beautiful mosaic is Steven Sykes.

Along a short wide passage, at the top of a few steps, is the circular Chapel of Christ the Servant. It is the centre for the Industrial Chaplains' work and is also known as the Chapel of Industry. The altar is a small oak slab on four white supports, standing on a round stone table engraved with the words, 'I am amongst you as One that serves.' Suspended above it is a huge Crown of Thorns. Through the circular glass walls there is a view of grass and trees and the sanctuary end of the ruin. Again I found myself looking respectfully, as at some interesting work of art in a modern exhibition; for me, despite the Crown of Thorns, it had nothing to do with religion; whereas the Chapel of Christ in Gethsemane I found profoundly moving, aesthetically and as expressing the very heart of redemption through sacrifice.

Returning to the cathedral and going down past the Tablets of the Word you come to the enormous baptistry window designed by John Piper, a glory of stained glass and stone impossible to describe. The designs in the lights are abstract, but the whole is intended to express the Light of the Holy Spirit. The centre part of the great curved structure is golden— a heavenly radiance; surrounding it are rich reds and greens and blues, and these colours are reflected in the polished marble slab on which rests the font, which is a huge rough boulder from a hillside near Bethlehem, untouched except to scallop a shallow basin at the top to hold the water. It arrived in Coventry on Christmas Eve, 1960, and for this three-ton Christmas gift from the Holy Land no charge was made at any stage of its delivery. 'Thus,' observes the Provost, 'the most modern cathedral has the most ancient font, and a physical link with "the Rock from which we are hewn".'

If you turn to the left when you leave the cathedral after the tour of the interior and go along the wide porch you come to St. Michael's Steps and find on the rose-red sandstone wall between them and the baptistry window the magnificent bronze Epstein sculpture of St. Michael triumphant over the

Devil. The Devil lies on his back with his hands and his ankles shackled and St. Michael's left foot on his forehead. The figure of the saint is winged and has a fine feeling of strength and movement characteristic of Epstein's winged carvings. This truly noble work was the last of Epstein's religious sculptures. The warm colour of the wall to which it is fixed harmonises with the darker sandstone of the ruins at the other side of the steps. The twentieth century and the fourteenth meet and merge in a noble unity.

Retracing your steps back along the porch you come to a curiously shaped blue stone building which forms a kind of annexe of the cathedral. It has the appearance of a round tower with a conical roof, encircled by tall flat slabs of buttresses. This is the Chapel of Unity, and the entrance is through the cathedral. Its curious shape is designed to give an impression of a crusader's tent. The chapel is dedicated to the unity of the Christian Churches. Its stained-glass windows, slit-like between tall interior buttresses, were designed by Margaret Traherne and were the gift of the German Evangelical churches. The marble mosaic floor, in the form of a ten-point Star of Bethlehem, was designed by Einar Forseth and given by the people of Sweden. Inset in the floor at the entrance is the inscription: *That they may all be one.* A black cross suspended above the circular table at the centre of the star signifies mourning for the division of the Church. The dove surrounded by flames in the middle of the star is symbolic of the Holy Spirit, and other Christian symbols are to be made out in the marble mosaic. On the floor in the doorway are the symbols of Christ's Passion— the Chalice, the Cross, the Crown of Thorns. For me it is all too light and bright, like the Chapel of Christ the Servant—the Chapel of Industry—but it is imaginatively conceived.

Beyond the Chapel of Unity, where Cuckoo Lane cuts across between Holy Trinity Church and the precincts of St. Michael's, beautiful with blossom-trees, you come to a narrow cobbled lane, little more than an alleyway, called Hill Top, and a short way down on the left-hand side is the small modern building which is the youth hostel, John Kennedy House, though it is difficult to get much idea of it from the lane.

A spiral staircase leads to the top of the spire of the old cathedral; it is a popular ascent, but not liking spiral staircases I did not make it, but instead sat for a while in the wide open space of the ruins watching the children and pigeons and strollers, and in the bright sunshine, and with so many camera-slung visitors, there was a sudden, fugitive reminiscence of the scene in the Piazza San Marco of Venice.

Some people say that though there are many beautiful things in the new Coventry Cathedral they do not add up to the unity necessary to a church. Perhaps it is a valid criticism; for the traditionalist it must all be entirely unacceptable, and perhaps it is too light and bright and un-private a place to pray in; but then there is the Lady Chapel, and the lovely little Chapel of Christ in Gethsemane, and anyone who could not pray in the latter I would think could not pray anywhere. For the un-believer, who does not pray but likes sometimes to meditate, there could be no more sympathetic place—during a service, of course, when visitors were not wandering about.

I had gone to Coventry with an open mind; I had no idea whether I would like this much-discussed cathedral or not; in general I do not much care for modern architecture—or so-called architecture, a good deal of which, square blocks of glass and cement, is non-architecture. I had been told that 'it grows on one, even when you hate it at first', and that 'it has nothing to do with religion'—but this last is nonsense; it has everything to do with religion, from the Charred Cross in the sanctuary in the ruins to the superlatively magnificent baptistry window—'a blaze of light, framed and islanded in colour'. I don't know who said it, but it's true; a blaze of light, and a glory inde-scribable. It could be painted, or expressed in music, perhaps, but not adequately in words.

For me, Coventry Cathedral was an intensely exciting

aesthetic experience, and in the deepest sense a religous one. I was impressed by the artistic vision of its creator, Sir Basil Spence, and moved by that other vision, the spiritual vision, of those who could see in this tremendous creation a medium for the expression of the supreme spiritual values of forgiveness and reconciliation.

I made two visits to Coventry, and on the second, with my daughter, went a little further afield, in search of the remains of the city's ancient walls and gates. These are only a short distance down the main street from Holy Trinity Church, close to the theatre, and are contained in a lovely small public garden called Lady Herbert's Garden. The first gate is at the entrance to the garden, the Stanswell Gate, and the second one, Cook Street Gate, at the other end of the garden. A notice in the archway of the Cook Street Gate says that there were twelve of these gates, which are fifteenth century, and only these two remain. The walls were destroyed by order of Charles II in 1662—a punishment twenty years late because during the Civil War the city had been a parliamentary stronghold, and in 1642 had refused to admit Charles I and his army.

There is an early fifteenth-century building, St. Mary's Hall, near the cathedral; it is considered to be one of the finest mediaeval guildhalls in the country, and at the other side of the city there are fifteenth-century almshouses, damaged during the blitz but restored; these I did not see, because one cannot do everything, but they constitute a good reason for making yet another visit to the valiant City of the Three Spires.

8

Maritime Bristol

MY first visit to Bristol was in the 'thirties, during the Spanish
Civil War, when I was working with Emma Goldman to make
known the little-known facts of the anarchist revolution behind the anti-Fascist struggle against Franco. Two or three of us,
headed by the old war-horse, Red Emma, had come up from
London for an evening meeting to enlighten the citizens of
Bristol. Of the meeting itself, over thirty years ago, I remember
nothing at all; it was merely one of a series up and down the
country; Emma, I suppose, would have ranted about 'Sta-
alin's henchmen', the sufferings of the 'Spa-anish people', and
the wickedness of the British and their policy of non-inter-
vention, and I, at the end of the tirade, would have had the
thankless task of 'making the appeal'. But of the place in which
we were put up for the night I have a very clear recollection, and
it was this memory which thirty years later drew me back to
Bristol for a closer inspection.

Our hostess was an elderly woman anarchist who lived alone
in a wooden chalet-style house on the wooded heights of
Clifton, above the Avon Gorge. Because she was elderly and
alone she had done nothing to the land which surrounded the
house, with the result that it was a sea of long grass—a 'rising
tide of grass', she called it, but provided she could get in and out
of her front and back doors it did not worry her—she seemed

even to like being islanded in this green sea. And it did have a
certain charm, for you could wade through it, knee deep, to the
edge of the cliffs above the gorge, and this was somehow romantic in the way that crossing a lawn could never be. Why,
after all, should an anarchist conform to conventional gardening
notions? It all, anyhow, seemed most wonderful, and for
a long time afterwards I coveted just such a house above the
Avon Gorge. In the morning, when we stood on the famous
suspension bridge, on our way back to the railway station and
the London train, I thought I had never seen so magnificent a
view as that deep wooded gorge. But when we had looked
sufficiently we got back into the car and drove on into Bristol
and I returned to London knowing no more than that.

Yet always at the back of my mind something insisted that
Bristol was a fine city. My interest in it was revived in recent
years when writing about Thomas Chatterton,[1] who was born
there and lived there until, in the manner of talented young
men of his time, he went to seek fame and fortune in London,
only to die there by his own hand at the age of seventeen. The
beautiful old church of St. Mary Redcliffe was his favourite
childhood haunt, and in due course he passed off his 'Rowley'
manuscripts on the scholars and antiquarians of his day—
including Horace Walpole—as the work of an unknown
Bristol priest of the days of Henry VI, which he claimed to have
found in an ancient chest in the muniments room of the church.
He had a pauper's burial in London, but there is a monument to
him in the churchyard of St. Mary Redcliffe. When I came to
plan this book it seemed natural to include Bristol in the proposed itinerary. I was resolved that this time I would really see
Bristol, maritime Bristol, the city of the Merchant Venturers.

It was a cold sunny morning in early March when I set out,
and from the train window the Wiltshire countryside, gently
undulating, was green with spring and there were black and
white cattle and frisking March lambs; all was serene and

1. In *Loneliness*, 1966.

unbuilt-on and 'swinging England' seemed another country.

Then Bath, rising in tiers of faded old yellow houses, with the spires of churches thrusting up everywhere, and swans on the river. From the train window there is discernible huge lettering on a grey roof: CHRIST DIED FOR OUR SINS. WE HAVE REDEMPTION THROUGH HIS BLOOD.

I had been in Bath many years ago, and I remembered it as a handsome, distinguished town, but I had no desire to revisit it, not much caring for the atmosphere of spas anywhere, finding it elderly and staid, and full of affliction, and somewhat steamy and mentally and physically suffocating, withal; and Bath is, in fact, a little airless, at the bottom of its bowl of hills; airless and sleepy—and genteel. My feeling inclines more to the vitality and movement of towns and cities that take life in their stride rather than in retirement. I have great sympathy for the Victorian songster who declared, iconoclastically:

Covent Garden Opera is all very fine,
Covent Garden Market is more my line!

Similarly the bustling port city of Bristol is more my line than the Regency elegance of Bath. John Betjeman, writing of ports in his little book, *English Cities and Small Towns*,[1] said that for him the best port of all was Bristol, which he saw as the 'capital of another kingdom, the West of England'. He found it possessed of more character than any city in England, and added, 'It keeps itself to itself.' He wrote in 1933; he might not think so now, for though it is still a fine city terrible things have been allowed to happen to it in recent years, despite all the efforts of its citizens. It can no longer be said to keep itself to itself, for on a tide of redevelopment and post-war reconstruction it has been swept into the main stream of contemporary life, and tall square blocks stand disconcertingly in places where they ought not.

1. Britain in Pictures Series, 1933.

But let us begin at the beginning, which for present purposes is Temple Meads Station, a remarkable castellated affair with 'battlements' and mullioned windows, early nineteenth century and choicest pseudo-Tudor. Pevsner observes of it that 'as a rule the Victorians had more sense, though that is now not always acknowledged'. The station cafeteria, named after Cabot, presents a similarly absurd masquerade, but it is all carried out in the lovely sandstone of which Bristol is built—until it reaches the glass and cement of the twentieth century—and once the absurdity is accepted has the make-believe appeal of an old-fashioned stage-set.

In the station yard I boarded a 'bus for the City Centre, though had I known how near it was I would have walked, taking in the great church of St. Mary Redcliffe on the way.

I wanted first to find King Street, famous for its seventeenth-century houses, including the Llandoger Trow Inn, the date of which is 1664, but a citizen of whom I inquired the way when I got off the 'bus immediately assumed I was in search of the Theatre Royal, the oldest active theatre in the country, built in 1776. The theatre is so small that except for the posters outside, announcing at that time *The Way of All Flesh*, being presented by the Bristol Old Vic Company, it would have been easy to pass it by, the eye more readily taken by the half-timbered seventeenth-century buildings flanking it. Across from it is the famous old inn, named by a Welsh trader who came from North Wales to Bristol in a boat of that name, and who bought the inn and re-named it, after his boat, the *Llandoger Trow*. It was connected with the slave trade, for which Bristol was famous, and the remains of a subterranean passage leading to the water suggests that it was used by smugglers.

On the same side of the street as the theatre are the St. Nicholas almshouses, bearing the date, 1656, and restored by the trustees in 1961. Outside a dark, half-timbered house of the same date, now a restaurant, baskets of plastic daffodils swung in the cold March wind—which they did not take with beauty.

Beyond the long low gabled façade of the almshouses, sand-wiched between them and the little theatre, rises a handsome eighteenth-century building, Cooper's Hall, designed by William Halfpenny in 1744. This narrow cobbled street is truly what it officially is, Bristol's 'Museum Street'. It ends at the river, with its Floating Harbour and its confusion of wharves and warehouses, and rising behind, starkly intruding, the high square block of the inescapable Robinson Building, a fifteen-storey office block completed in 1963.

Turning my back on this late twentieth-century intrusion I retraced my steps along the street and came to some more alms-houses, built by the Merchant Venturers for seamen and their widows in 1696. They are built round three sides of a square laid out as a garden, and are hemmed in by modern office blocks. On a board on the upper part of the almshouse facing across the little garden to the street the following verse is inscribed in a neat script:

> Freed from all storms and tempests' rage
> Of billows, here we spend our age.
> Our weather-beaten vessels here renew,
> And from the Merchants' kind and generous care
> End labour here. No more we put to sea
> Until we launch into eternity.
>
> And lest our Widows whom we leave behind
> Should want relief they too a shelter find.
> Thus all our anxious cares and sorrows cease,
> Whilst our kind Guardians turn our trials to ease.
> May they be with an endless sabbath blest
> Who have afforded us this rest.

In those days, it is clear, the Poor were expected to show a proper gratitude to their benefactors—in this case those rich merchants who grew fat on the slave trade, the import of wine,

tobacco, sugar, and later, in the eighteenth century, the manufacture of porcelain, glass, chocolate. The Society of Merchant
Venturers was founded in 1552, but their heyday came later,
when the new trade routes began to open up. The decline of
the merchant princes set in in the eighteenth century and continued into the nineteenth. Various things contributed to it—
the emancipation of the slaves in the West Indies in the 1830's
and the consequent loss of that trade (the slaves were bought in
West Africa and sold there, and Bristol led in this shameful
trade), the rise of Liverpool, the heavy rates levied by the Bristol
Dock Company to pay for the Floating Harbour built in 1809,
but the abolition of the slave trade was the chief factor in the
decline.

Across the road from King Street you come to the wide and
grassy open space of College Green, flanked at one side by the
mediaeval and nineteenth-century Cathedral Church of the
Holy and Undivided Trinity, and at the far side by the long
curved sweep of the modern—1955—civic building known as
the Council House. The cathedral was once the Abbey of St.
Augustine, founded by Robert Fitzhardinge in 1142; a Norman
gateway and the chapter house of the abbey remain. The building of the Council House cost Bristol its City Cross and was a
subject of controversy. It has costly gilded unicorns perched
on its roof at either end, and at ground level, facing the lawns
of the Green, and behind a fountain, a statue of John Cabot,
designed by Sir Charles Wheeler. The building was begun in
1936 and opened by the Queen in 1956. It was designed by
E. Vincent Harris, and is handsome, in the modern idiom.
Behind it the Cabot Tower, tall and square, rises above trees on
Brandon Hill.

Park Street, Bristol's 'Bond Street', leads up steeply from the
Council House, to the university, with its fine Oatley tower,
designed by Sir George Oatley, and which Pevsner calls a
'*tour de force* in Gothic revival, so convinced, so vast, and so
competent that one cannot help feeling respect for it'. The

City Museum and Art Gallery adjoin the university, and from here there is a view out over the city.

Across the road and up a winding lane, past a square of stately eighteenth-century houses, Berkeley Square, and an alleyway called There-and-Back-Again-Lane, you come to the public gardens of Brandon Hill. The tower was erected to commemorate the fourth centenary of the voyage of John Cabot from Bristol to North America. A path winds up through shrubs and trees to the terrace at the base of the tower, and there are fine views, one way out over the countryside, with low wooded hills in the near distance, and the other out over the city with its church spires and modern blocks. A turnstile gives access to a spiral staircase which leads to the top of the tower, but the interior was dark, and I did not feel moved to make the ascent.

Instead, I made my way back down Brandon Hill, through the blossoming almond trees and past drifts of daffodils in the grass, to College Green, and on from there to Queen's Square, flanked by the noble houses once inhabited by the merchant princes. It is a place of grass and trees, like the great London squares, and has the same dignified beauty. It was designed at the end of the seventeenth century as part of an expansionist programme, the city by then bursting at its seams from increased population. On old maps it is shown, with King Street, as 'Ye Marsh'.

At the other side of this fine square you come quickly to a small and ugly iron bridge, the Redcliffe Bridge, and behind old warehouses beside the river rise modern blocks, and towering over them all the Robinson building; but across the bridge, on the other side, rises what is perhaps Bristol's greatest treasure, the Church of St. Mary Redcliffe, on the low ridge of red cliffs above the river and the docks, at the heart of maritime Bristol. This most beautiful and cathedral-like church was founded in the twelfth century, but was rebuilt by William Canynges in the fourteenth and completed by his grandson in the fifteenth. In those years the merchant seamen of the port began and ended their voyages at the Shrine of Our Lady of Redcliffe. Canon R. F. Cartwright, vicar, is interesting on this; in his admirable history of the church,[1] he says: 'Seafarers would make their way from the harbour to the church, enter the porch by the west door, make their offering and leave by the east door. The most famous to be associated with St. Mary Redcliffe were John and Sebastian Cabot, who set sail from Bristol in 1497, and discovered Newfoundland. On their return they brought the rib of a cow whale, which hangs in the church under the tower. At one time they lived in Cathay, a picturesque street to the south-east of the church, demolished in 1960.'

In the tower, also, is a painted wooden figure of Queen Elizabeth I, believed to be contemporary, and to have been a ship's figurehead, which it does indeed look like. The first Queen Elizabeth called St. Mary Redcliffe the 'fairest, goodliest, and most famous Parish Church in England'.

The main entrance is through the wonderful north porches—there are two, outer and inner. The outer porch has been described as 'one of the loveliest "Decorated" rooms in all England; hexagonal in shape, and more glorious than its only rival at Ludlow'. Externally the stonework of the porch is richly and elaborately carved, and the doors have a Moorish appearance. Over the porch is the muniments room associated with Chatterton; the church's documents are now housed in a special strong room, but the ancient chests remain. What does not remain, I am sorry to report, is the monument to Chatterton which used to stand at the north-east corner of the churchyard, surmounted by a statue of him wearing the uniform of the blue-coat school he attended for eight years. I had particularly wanted to see this statue, but a deacon of whom I inquired told me that the monument had been removed at the beginning of the year, 1967, as it was decaying; he is now commemorated

1. *The Pictorial History of St. Mary Redcliffe, Bristol*, Pitkin Pictorials, 1963.

only by a small dark marble lozenge-shaped tablet in the church, close to the elaborate tomb of William Canynges and his wife, at the south side. All that is inscribed on the plaque is: *Thomas Chatterton of this Parish, 1752–1770. Poet.*

Facing the south door of the church a tombstone lying on the grassy slope commemorates the boy-poet's parents; his father is described as a 'poor schoolmaster', who died in 1752—Thomas was born three months later.

Close to this slab is a small stone tombstone, also lying on the grass, in memory of *The Church Cat, 1912–1927.*

But to return to the wonderful interior of the church: the tower windows contain mediaeval glass, pale and delicate in the west window, vivid in the north one. The tower-space was furnished as a chapel in 1965, as the result of gifts received from American Friends of St. Mary Redcliffe. The inner north porch, from which one passes to the tower, is the oldest part of the building, and was the entrance to the twelfth-century church. It is regarded as a gem of early English architecture. It contains slender black shafts of Purbeck marble, and beautiful stone carving.

High up on the wall of the tower, opposite the baptistry, hang the armour and gauntlets of Admiral Sir William Penn, father of the Quaker Penn who founded Pennsylvania, together with his sword and shield, and the pennants of his ships engaged in the Dutch wars. Below this array there is a tablet on which his history has been set forth by his son—but at that height it is not readable.

The octagonal stone font is medieval; close to it is another font, eighteenth century and alabaster, tall and graceful, like an elegant vase.

The beautiful wrought-iron and gilded gates beneath the tower are also eighteenth century; they were made by William Edney of Bristol in 1710 as a screen for the chancel; the arms at the top are those of the city of Bristol, and they are surmounted by the scales of justice.

There are great treasures, also, at the other end of the church. In the north choir aisle there is the beautiful fifteenth-century tomb of Philip Mede and his family. Philip Mede was three times mayor of Bristol. The tomb is double, under an elaborately carved stone canopy: in the western half effigies of Philip Mede and his wife lie side by side; in the other half a fine square brass depicts their son Richard and his two wives. To the right of the tomb is the Handel window, erected a hundred years after his death; it is carried out in soft colours and shows Jesus as the Good Shepherd, with lambs abounding; the eight panels represent passages from the *Messiah*. Handel was a close friend of the vicar of that time, and revised some of his oratorios on the organ which stood then at the west end of the church.

In a glass case nearby is a copy of the Geneva Bible—the so-called 'Breeches Bible', which renders Genesis iii, 7, 'And they sewed fig tree leaves together and made themselves breeches.'

The east window of the Lady Chapel, behind the high altar, is modern, by a contemporary artist, Mr. H. J. Stammers. It is carried out in harsh blues, reds, yellows, and depicts scenes from the life of Jesus, but at the bottom left there are figures in modern dress. In the side windows there are both modern and mediaeval figures, and a nude female figure (Eve?) and females in what would appear to be topless dresses. . . .

In the south transept there is the tomb of William Canynges the Younger, five times Mayor of Bristol, and his wife, the painted effigies lying side by side, splendidly apparelled, Canynges in the robes of a rich merchant; the tomb is like a huge four-poster; just beyond it is another effigy of Canynges, in alabaster, depicting him in the robes of a priest, which he became after his wife's death. He is described on the memorial tablet as '*a great man, a great merchant venturer, and a great benefactor of St. Mary Redcliffe*'.

It is necessary to go along the balustraded walk at the west side of the churchyard to appreciate the significance of the

Redcliffe in the name of the church. Approaching the church from the railway station and entering by the north porch you are not aware that it stands on a ridge above the river, but at the end of the balustraded walk you look down Redcliffe Hill, flanked at one side by a terrace of shabby Georgian houses, once the homes of rich merchants, and there is a view out across the docks and shipping to the Somerset hills—with the inevitable high block in the near distance. Between the church and the houses stands the old Shot Tower.

Below the balustraded walk, at the side of the street's narrow pavement, there is a very interesting water pipe projecting from an archway a few feet above the pavement; it is interesting not only because of the strange animal's head which surmounts the pipe but because of the history of this strange conduit. In 1190 Lord Robert de Berkeley gave to the church his Ruge (ridge) Well and conduit, together with the right for it to be piped across the lands to the people of Redcliffe. The spring rises at Knowle and is piped through Lower Knowle and Bedminster to Redcliffe, where it is to be seen in the pool below the balustraded walk, where the animal's-head pipe projects from the small archway. Every year the church asserts its rights to the water-supply by organising a walk 'the whole length of the Pipe to its source in Knowle with lively ceremony'.

The narrow streets that once surrounded the church have been swept away in that relentless tide of 'progress' which expresses itself in multi-storey blocks of flats and offices, but despite this, and the devastation of air-raids in World War II, a surprising amount of old Bristol does remain. There is even a scrap of the medieval wall at St. John's Gate, between Broad Street and Bell Lane; this is the only remaining gate of the city's nine, and over it is built the little church of St. John the Baptist, known as St. John's-on-the-Walls, the date of which, according to a plaque on the wall, is 1174. A notice-board announces that visitors are welcome but, alas, the door was locked, so I cannot report on the interior, but apparently it is very narrow, being only the width of the wall. Below it are three archways, the main body of the church, with its square tower and tall spire, being over the centre one. On the Bell Lane side there are painted and gilded seated figures, possibly of Norman earls. The church is hemmed in by high-rise buildings —but this is true of so many of Bristol's churches, unfortunately.

At the end of Bell Lane you come to the big reconstruction area, flanked at one side by the modern building of the Norwich Union and at the other by the Bank of England, opened in 1963; both these modern buildings have ruined church towers behind them. Great controversy was aroused over the erection of these commercial buildings in this area, which Bristolians had understood was to be rebuilt for purely civic purposes; 11,000 citizens signed a petition of protest against the proposed commercial buildings, but they went up all the same, with high square blocks behind. It is all the sadder because here, until the blitz, stood the beautiful seventeenth-century Dutch House, which Pevsner calls the finest of the city's timber houses, and close by the twelfth-century church of St. Mary-le-Port, the ruined tower of which is being made safe for preservation, though it rises now, incongruously, between the Norwich Union and the Bank of England.

This area was once the hub of Bristol, and up here is the handsome eighteenth-century Corn Exchange, designed by John Wood the Elder. In front of it stand what at first sight appear to be capstans, but which are in fact the famous Brass Nails—short pillars with flat tops on which money was paid out; hence the expression 'paying on the nail'. Two of them are Elizabethan; the other two are dated 1625 and 1631. Behind the Exchange is a covered flower and fruit market, leading into narrow All Saints Lane. Here all is old and quietly pleasing, but cross a road and descend some steps and come again to the river and you are once again confronted with the ubiquitous Robinson building.

The real City Centre is the Tram Centre, where the River Frome has been covered over and gardens with grass and flowers have been laid out, and the old Tramways Office, with its famous clock, is now a bus and coach services office.

World War II took a great deal from Bristol, and modern 'development' has intruded brutally upon what remains, but in spite of all Bristol is still a fine old city, a *maritime* city, with a fugitive smell of the sea about it, and the feeling that the docks and shipping and city are one, crowned by the Perpendicular beauty of the church of St. Mary on its ridge of red cliffs above the Avon, the church which houses a ship's figurehead and the bone of a whale, and in which merchant princes and the men who sailed their ships began and ended their voyages at the shrine of Our Lady of Redcliffe. The multi-storey blocks and towers have encroached because Bristol is also a commercial city, but first and last it is a port, with its own maritime individuality. What Betjeman wrote in 1933 is still true, despite all that has happened since—the devastation of the war, the 'development' and reconstruction of the post-war—'the strong character is not destroyed nor have all its best buildings and its narrow steep alleyways disappeared. Bristol will never die.'

9

Walled Cities: Chester and York

FROM my childhood, and the pictures in the fairy-tale books, walled cities have fascinated me. Carcassonne was a persistent dream, but I did not get there until the late 'thirties. The Breton walled city of St. Malo I did not see until the 'fifties. Carcassonne is a miracle of restoration; St. Malo had to be restored, too, after the Second World War, though the twelfth-century ramparts were untouched by the bombs of the liberation. Many times I walked round the walls of St. Malo before I set foot on the walls of Chester and York, those capital cities of old England; these had to wait until I was working on this book in the spring of 1967.

Yet I had dreamed of the walls of Chester incessantly, because for many years I was sending films to be developed and printed by a Chester firm with an address in Bridge Street Row. I knew about the famous Rows, yet could somehow no more visualise them than I could the two and a half miles of intact walls enclosing the city. Could one really walk round the walls of Chester and York as one could round the ramparts of Carcassonne and St. Malo? I could not imagine it; I persuaded myself that there were probably only short broken stretches of wall.

On a cold windy day in April I discovered that the walls of Chester are intact; if you go up the steps of the Eastgate, which is on the main shopping street of the city, near the cathedral, and start walking, and keep on, inside the hour you will be back where you started, having circuited the city. It is a very pleasant walk, too, and affords the only really satisfactory view of the cathedral. Soon after passing the cathedral you come to a round tower called King Charles' Tower, in the north-east angle of the wall. It is part of the Roman fortress, but has been called by its present name ever since September 24, 1645, when Charles I stood there and watched the defeat of his army at Rowton Moor. In the summer it is open as a museum. Looking north the view out over the countryside to distant hills, beyond the city, is very fine; without binoculars, however, King Charles could hardly have watched the progress of a battle at that distance; it must have been fought much nearer in: there was then, of course, no city beyond the walls.

Still traversing the Roman wall you come next to the Northgate, but this present gate was built as recently as 1810, replacing a mediaeval structure which had dungeons beneath. The Roman wall ends a little farther along at the Goblin Tower, which is like a tower sliced down the middle; another name for it is Pemberton's Parlour, so-called after John Pemberton, a rope-maker and Mayor of Chester in 1730, who used it as a vantage point to watch his workmen on the rope-walk below. An earlier name for it was Dille's Tower, but who was Dille, and why he should have had a tower named after him, I do not know. After this the walls are of Saxon origin, and you come next to the curiously named Bonewaldesthorne's Tower in the north-west angle of the wall. It is an ancient round tower in the style of the King Charles' Tower, but with steps up to the entrance. Its name has apparently long puzzled antiquaries. It has been suggested that it was named after an Anglo-Saxon thane; another theory is that the name is derived from the Norse, the tower having overlooked the meeting place of a Norse 'Thing' or parliament.

From this north-west angle of the wall a massive spur runs

out to the beautiful old thirteenth-century Water Tower. There are yew trees here at the top of the wall, and below are some attractive gardens. In the summer this tower, also, is open as a museum. Before the River Dee receded this tower was a watch tower guarding the port of Chester on the estuary. Ships then anchored under the walls of the city. Mr. E. H. Mason, deputy director of Cheshire County Library and Museum, says in his Pitkin Pictorial booklet on Chester, 'The Danes had sailed up the river, founding communities in Wirral and even occupying the ruins of Chester itself when hotly pursued by the Saxons. King Edgar the Peaceable had sailed with a great fleet from the Severn to the Dee and so to Chester. From the twelfth to the fourteenth centuries the port enjoyed its most prosperous period, especially in trading with Ireland. . . .' There were also imports from France and Spain, and ships sailing from Chester carried cargoes of cheese and salt, gloves and candles. The mayor of Chester bore the title of Admiral of the Dee, and 'up to the end of the sixteenth century', says Mr. Mason, 'Liverpool was looked upon by Cestrians as being "but a creek of the port of Chester" '.

During the fifteenth century, however, the estuary began to silt up, 'and instead of merchant ships tying up by the Water Gate at the foot of Watergate Street, they were forced to anchor some twelve miles down stream'. The trade of the port naturally declined and the city's prosperity suffered.

This is a very beautiful part of the wall, looking out over waterways and gardens and the countryside beyond the city, as it does, and once you have turned your back on the Water Tower and continue on along the western walls there is no more scenery. Here the top of the wall and the existing road at the left are on the same level; at the other side, below, is the big race-course called the Roodee, where horse races have been held since 1540. The name is derived from two Anglo-Saxon words, *rood* meaning cross, and *eye* meaning island; the great green arena of over sixty acres is the island of the cross, and there is still the base of an old stone cross in the middle of it.

At the end of the Roodee the wall breaks and a busy motor-road drives through to the famous Grosvenor Bridge across the river. This bridge was designed by a famous Chester architect, Thomas Harrison, who died a few years before it was opened in 1832 by the young Princess Victoria, who became queen five years later. At the time, the 200-foot span of the main arch of the bridge was the greatest single span of any stone arch in the world and was a remarkable feat of engineering. It is still a handsome bridge and the area beyond is wooded and beautiful.

If instead of going along to the bridge you cross the road you pick up the wall again, following it round past the castle. All that is left of the ancient castle is a thirteenth-century tower; the castellated structure surmounting a grassy knoll above the walls is comparatively modern. I was sorry that just before going to Chester I had read Pamela Hansford Johnson's book, *On Iniquity*,[1] which she wrote as a result of her few days' attendance at the unspeakable Moors Murders trial which was held at the Assize courts housed in the castle. I was sorry because as soon as the castle came into view I remembered. As Miss Hansford Johnson says in her book, so fine a city as Chester deserved a better fate than the infection of that horror. But when you have passed the castle you come to the handsome modern building of the County Hall, constructed of natural stone, and brick, and overlooking the river, with boats and swans and cascades, and the memory of horror and evil recedes. The County Hall was begun in 1938, but, interrupted by the war, was not finished until 1957, when it was opened by the Queen.

Continuing on you cross the Bridgegate, built in the late eighteenth century to replace a mediaeval gate which, according to the tablet, had 'long been inconvenient'. You mount some steps and are on the east walls again, and the last lap of the Saxon walls; at Newgate the Roman wall begins, and a short

1. 1967.

distance beyond is the Eastgate by the cathedral, completing the circuit. Newgate has a mediaeval appearance, with its towers, but was in fact built in 1938; below it are gardens with Roman remains, where some reconstruction is going on. The Romans, it seems, knew all about underfloor heating, as shown here. A passage-way from the wall here leads to a covered, pedestrian shopping centre, warm and airless with its glass roof, leading out into an arcade, and the fresh air of St. Michael's Street. It is only a few yards from here along the wall to Eastgate, or you can leave the wall there and explore the Rows.

The Rows are shops at first-floor level, above those at pavement level, and are, really, a series of arcades open at one side on to the street. At intervals there are steps up from the pavement. These first-floor arcades are on Watergate Street and Eastgate Street, the main shopping thoroughfares, which cut across the city west–east, with the late eighteenth-century Water Gate at one end and the Eastgate, on the Roman wall, at the other. There are Rows, also, on Bridge Street running southward to the river. The buildings of which the Rows form the first floor are black and white seventeenth century, timbered, some of them with elaborate wood-carvings. Some of them, now inns, were once the town houses of the nobility. It is a great pity that here and there a hideous modern building has been allowed to squeeze its concrete-and-glass squareness in between these fine old buildings. There is a shocking example of this on Eastgate Street. Why doesn't Chester cherish and protect itself as what it in effect is—an ancient monument?

Outside the walls there are some very beautiful gardens, Grosvenor Park, going down to the river. The Suspension Bridge is here, and between it and Grosvenor Bridge the Old Dee Bridge, built in the fourteenth century. Charles I escaped over this bridge into North Wales after the defeat of his army at Rowton Moor. The wooded riverside walks are called the Groves and are very pleasant.

It is pleasant, too, in the narrow streets round the cathedral, which was originally the eleventh-century Benedictine abbey of St. Werburgh. The street of old houses facing the cathedral is called St. Werburgh Street, and there is Abbey Square, once the courtyard of the abbey, behind the cathedral and surrounded by eighteenth-century houses, with the bishop's house tucked away in a corner. The fourteenth-century Abbey Gateway leads into the square.

The oldest part of the cathedral is the north transept, built shortly after the Battle of Hastings; there is a Norman arch and gallery, and all is dark and sombre. Very beautiful is an Early English wall-pulpit built into the wall under an arcade of stone arches in a part of the cathedral which was once the refectory of the abbey; it is reached through an arched doorway and up a small stone staircase under the arcade. From it, in the old days, a monk read to his brethren at meal times. The elaborately carved fourteenth-century canopied stalls of the choir are extremely beautiful and are one of the chief treasures of the cathedral. The stained glass is modern, nineteenth century, and some early twentieth. The window of St. Werburga—as the name is rendered there—in the cloisters is twentieth century. The cathedral was extensively restored by Sir Gilbert Scott in the nineteenth century, following decay in the sandstone; much of the exterior—pinnacles, flying buttresses, turrets—is all new work by him. Work has been put in on the cathedral in every century from the twelfth to the present day. The south front of the south transept is by Thomas Harrison, who designed the Grosvenor Bridge.

I did not have time, and was also too tired after all the walking round the walls and in the city, to take in more of the cathedral than I have indicated in the foregoing notes; England has finer cathedrals, and Chester Cathedral is, to my mind, best viewed from the Roman wall at Eastgate through a screen of blossoming cherry trees, across the beautiful war memorial garden dedicated to the 22nd (Cheshire) Regiment.

At Coventry and at Bristol, when you arrive by train you take a 'bus from the station yard to the City Centre; at Chester you walk down a rather dreary street to Eastgate; but at York when you emerge from the railway station the glory of the walls is there, confronting you, pale grey ramparts topping the grass-covered slopes of the moat, in spring cloth-of-gold with daffodils, which was how I saw it. If you are not prepared for it, and I was not, the unexpected splendour is startling. So beautiful, and all there—not to be searched for. Away to the left, and excitingly near, are the pinnacled twin towers of the cathedral with the massive square central tower behind. Your heart sings—well, if it is a foolish, excitable heart like mine. All this and the Minster too. . . .

But resolutely I turned my back on the Minster and marched off under the walls to the gate I wanted, the Micklegate Bar. I knew there was not going to be time to make the complete circuit of the walls, nearly three miles, and see all else that I wanted to see, and having done my homework before I set out I knew that if there could only be one stretch of the wall this, which would face the cathedral all the way, was it. Sometime I hope to revisit York and complete the circuit of the walls as I did at Chester. According to the Official Guide the most popular section of the walls is from Bootham Bar, at the other side of the river, near the cathedral, to Monk Bar, forming a triangle; beyond the Monk Bar the wall goes on to meet the River Foss, which interrupts it. (It should be explained that York has four great gates—Micklegate Bar, to the south, Bootham Bar, to the west, Monk Bar, to the north, and Walmgate Bar to the east, beyond the Foss. They date from the thirteenth century and were the strongest points in the walls, commanding the main roads to the city—which they still do. The most important was Micklegate Bar, traditionally the gate by which the king entered the city. A great deal of mediaeval pageantry flowed in through this gate, and in the course of history many a severed head has decorated the top. . . .)

The walk along the walls from Micklegate Bar is very beautiful, with the grassy slopes of the moat going down to lovely public gardens, and on the other side grassy banks descending to the road, and where that stretch of wall ends, at Lendal Bridge, more gardens. There is no parapet on the inside of the walls, but wherever a road cuts through there are protective railings.

The river view at Lendal Bridge, the stretch known as the Guildhall Reach, is quite astonishingly Venetian, for here, as in Venice, the buildings stand with their feet in the water, and the Guildhall is a very handsome, palatial building. It was built in the fifteenth century, largely destroyed by fire bombs in 1942, carefully restored in recent years, and re-opened in 1960. The stone for building the Minster was landed at the Guildhall watergate—in those days the River Ouse was an important waterway, like the Dee, and knew the ships of the Merchant Venturers, sailing for Europe with cargoes of wool.

From Lendal Bridge, Museum Street leads us to Duncombe Place and directly to the cathedral. At the junction of the two streets there is St. Leonard's Terrace, a fine Regency Terrace at the end of which is the old Theatre Royal, home of the York Repertory Company. The wall was breached here, in Georgian times, for the creation of this terrace; at the end of it is Bootham Bar, from which the wall continues on to Monk Bar. Petergate, the narrow, winding street of old houses and antique shops, immediately in front of the cathedral, follows the line of the Roman *via principalis*. Truly, as has been said, 'the history of York is the history of England'. Stonegate, off Petergate, was the *via praetoria*, leading to the headquarters of the Roman legions, and below it the original cobbled Roman road still exists, complete with its centre gulley for the chariots' skid wheels. The present-day street is not very attractive, being a confusion of mediaeval and eighteenth-century buildings, upon the façades of which ugly modern shop fronts have been imposed.

There are, however, a number of attractive old narrow streets in this area, including, of course, the famous Shambles, which is almost too picturesque to be true, with its fifteenth-century timbered houses with overhanging upper storeys leaning out across the cobblestones. As its name indicates, it was the street of the butchers, but is now mostly antique shops, souvenir shops, inns, though there are still, I noticed, some butchers' shops. Behind, there is an open-air market for fruit, vegetables, flowers, clothes, poultry and sea-food. A notice announces that when the bell rings at five-thirty all selling must instantly cease.

The Shambles leads out to what is now a modern commercial main street, with the usual chain stores, and a hideous concrete tiered car park at one end. Was that really necessary? The more so since the street itself, which is called the Pavement, was originally fifteenth century, and some medieval houses remain. To the left, on leaving the Shambles, is the curiously named Whip-ma-Whop-ma-gate. At the other end of the Shambles is another narrow street called Goodramgate, leading to Monk Bar, at one time called Goodramgate Bar; this street contains the oldest houses in York, thirteenth century, now a row of shops.

I retraced my steps to Petergate and before going into the Minster explored the other side of it, for the precincts of any cathedral are always interesting. You come immediately to the beautiful black-and-white half-timbered St. William's College, founded in 1461 for the chantry priests of the cathedral. At the Reformation it became a private house; during the Civil Wars, when York was a royalist centre, Charles I set up a printing press there. Later it became tenement dwellings. It was restored in 1900 and is now the meeting place of the York Convocation. When not in use it is open to the public.

The Treasurer's House lies behind. It is extremely beautiful. It stands on the site of the Roman Imperial Barracks, of which traces remain. The original house was the residence of the

Treasurer of the Minster, the first being appointed at the beginning of the twelfth century. The present house contains work
of the thirteenth century and is believed to have been rebuilt by
Archbishop John le Romeyne in the fourteenth. Part of it is now
used as an annexe to St. John's Training College. The house was
lived in continuously until 1930, when the last owner, Mr.
Frank Green, presented it to the National Trust.

It is only a shilling to go into St. William's College, but half
a crown to go into the Treasurer's House. Whilst I was standing
looking across the beautiful garden, with lawns and trees and
statuary, debating with myself not so much whether I would
spend the half-crown but whether I really had time to go in, a
man and woman came and stood beside me and read the notice-
board. 'Half a crown!' the woman exclaimed. 'Perhaps we'll
skip it!' said the man, and they went back the way they had
come, in the direction of St. William's College. Their decision
settled my own; I, too, decided to skip it and continued on
through the cathedral precincts, where there are notices warning you not to stand on the grassy banks, which cover water
cisterns and are not strong enough to withstand weight, and
you ignore the warning at your peril—'Danger of death'.
Pursued by an icy wind, which also seemed to threaten danger
of death, I came round again to the west front of the cathedral.
There was scaffolding everywhere, and notices to the public to
beware. This greatest of cathedrals really is falling down, and
inside whole areas are roped off from the public; the trepi-
dation I felt on entering, however, had nothing to do with this,
but everything to do with the feeling of utter inadequacy in the
presence of something so tremendous.

York Minster has been described as England's treasure house
of old glass. Its windows contain at least half the mediaeval
stained glass in the country. A. L. Laishley, in a very interesting
booklet entitled *The City of York*, published in York, says that
the nave of the cathedral 'contains the finest collection of
fourteenth-century glass in existence, and also a panel dating

from the twelfth century', adding that 'the Great East Window was created between the years 1405 and 1408 by the master glass painter John Thornton of Coventry, and is the largest window of its kind in the world'. This mediaeval glass is remarkable for the richness of its colours, deep reds and blues, and brilliant golds and greens, such as seem not to be reproduced to the same degree of intensity in modern glass.

The famous Five Sisters Window, in the north transept, however, and which dates from the thirteenth century, is something quite different; it is of a delicate grey-green, and is of a purely geometric design, no figures being depicted. It is of great grace and beauty, set in the long narrow lancet windows, each over fifty feet in depth and four feet in width, though they look so delicate and slender.

A person such as myself, knowing little of church architecture, can only be a totally inadequate guide to one of the world's greatest cathedrals; I can only report, humbly, on the splendour of the glass, and the almost overwhelming majesty and beauty of soaring archways and vaulted ceilings. There is the feeling of being in the presence of one of Man's truly noble creations.

Of great grace and beauty, too, are the ruins of St. Mary's Abbey Church in the beautiful Museum Gardens beside the river. The abbey was Benedictine and founded in 1080 was the first monastic house to be established in Yorkshire after the Norman Conquest. It was suppressed in 1540. The shell of the great Abbey Church, with its lofty entrance archway, is used for the mediaeval Mystery Plays performed as part of York's triennial Festival of Music and the Arts. There are also the remains of a guest-house and gatehouse, and the thirteenth-century walls of the precincts still stand. Part of the ruins of a round tower are fourth-century Roman; it was added to when it was incorporated into the medieval city walls. It is called the Multangular Tower, and was part of the Roman fortress of

Eboracum. In the handsome York Museum in the gardens, nineteenth century, with pillared portico, are many treasures excavated from Roman York, along with thirteenth- and fourteenth-century statues and carvings—a stone carving of the flight of the Holy Family into Egypt is pleasantly primitive.

A museum I did not have time to visit but which is of great importance and interest is across the road from here, on the same side of the river, the Castle Museum, one of the world's outstanding folk museums, opened in 1938. It was created by a famous antiquary, Dr. J. L. Kirk, who built it up very much as Sydney Cumbers (Captain 'Long John' Silver) built up his maritime museum, establishing it first, as the 'Cap'n' did, in his own home, and faced finally by a similar problem of accommodating the considerable collection it had become. By arrangement with the York Corporation the collection was finally housed in an eighteenth-century building which was formerly the Prison for Females; the original façade has been preserved and is scheduled as an ancient monument, and the interior was adapted in 1938 to the requirements of a modern museum. Dr. Kirk collected any-and-everything connected with the county of Yorkshire in bygone days. Thus in the museum there is a reproduction of a room in an old moorland cottage, with spinning-wheel, period furniture, kitchen utensils. There is a reproduction of a sweet shop of the days of this generation of children's great-grand-parents, and this exhibit is apparently immensely popular with the 80,000 or so school children who visit the museum every year, brought there in parties or attending in classes. There are Georgian and Regency shop fronts, with life-size figures of craftsmen of the period at work, and the products of their trades, and the tools and equipment used, are all exhibited. There is a reconstructed cobbled street called Kirkgate, after Dr. Kirk. The shops include a pewterer's, a coppersmith's, an apothecary's, a saddler's. In 1952 the adjoining building, known as the Debtors' Prison, built in 1705 by Sir John Vanbrugh, was opened as an extension to the Castle

Museum. According to the Official Guide, 'The latest addition to the Museum is a complete Edwardian street of shops including a "pub", an early motor garage, a gipsy caravan and the Sheriff's coach. The shop windows are filled with the latest household gadgets, drapery, gas mantles, straw hats and the wonder of the age—electricity.'

I had been recommended not to miss this museum, but I had lingered too long in the lovely gardens of the other museum, but it is always good to have an excuse to revisit a fine old city, and I would like to return to York and visit the Folk Museum with my little grand-daughter, who is of the right age—six years old—to bring to it the proper sense of wonder.

10

Chichester—via Butlin's

FOR anyone with a taste for contrast it is hardly possible to do better; on the one hand a garishness and fun-fair vulgarity almost beyond the power of words to describe, and on the other sixteenth-century grey stone, eighteenth-century red brick, a noble cathedral in a setting of grass and tress, flint houses, old walls, herbaceous borders, almshouses contained in a lofty raftered hall dating from the thirteenth century.

The weekend at the Butlin Holiday Camp at Bognor Regis had not been originally planned for the sake of contrast with Chichester, though I had always intended to visit Chichester, only a half hour's 'bus ride from Bognor, from there. I went to Butlin's in a spirit of 'research'; I was interested, curious. I had not expected to like it for the simple reason that I am too innately anarchist by temperament to take kindly to centralised organisation, and from my earliest years jollity has depressed me. On the eve of my departure a woman bookshop assistant told me that some friends of hers had gone, 'but they left next day— they couldn't stand it!' A woman bank cashier told me, 'We have some friends who go year after year to the one at Bognor. We asked them once, "Why don't you go to another one, for a change? Why not the one at Minehead?" But they said what was the point in going all that way, when they never went out of the camp, and Bognor was so near. . . .'

A woman friend and one-time neighbour, a Mrs. Kathleen Taylor, had offered to accompany me. I had protested, half teasing, half in earnest, 'But you wouldn't like it! You're gently nurtured and have lived a very sheltered life! It's different for an old hand like me that's knocked about all over the world!'

'It would be an experience,' she insisted. 'And now that I'm a widow and beginning to spread my wings a little . . .'

'All right,' I said, 'but you fill in the forms. I'm allergic to forms.'

So she filled in the forms, which demanded to know our ages, sex, married status, relationship to each other, ignoring the ribald suggestions I made for dealing with these highly personal inquiries; what *she* found shocking, apparently, was the note embodied in the forms requiring campers to bring their own soap and towels. What finally broke her up, however, was the goings-on in the chalet 'lines' when the happy campers finally left their 'late-night sing-song' in the so-called Regency bar at midnight and surged merrily back to their chalets; the rumpus, with shouts and shrieks and loutish laughter, and the clatter of dustbins being flung around, and a crash of broken glass, as an assault was made by some lively lads on the bathroom window of a chalet occupied by some giggling but protesting lasses, went on until 1.30 a.m. . . . (It should be explained that there are no men and women, boys and girls, at Butlin's; all are lads and lasses both in the loud-speakered announcements by the Redcoats and the indications on the W.C. doors.)

In the morning, lying staring at the dirty yellow paint of the roughcast walls of my chalet, and listening to the dulcet voice of someone who announced herself as Flo telling me over the Tannoy system that it was eight-thirty and that at nine my breakfast would be ready ('your' breakfast, and 'your' evening meal gives the subtle personal touch) I thought that if I were alone I would leave after breakfast for Chichester and then get a train back to London, but since Kathleen had so generously offered to spend this weekend with me here, had so wanted the experience, and the few days by the sea, such a plan would not be fair on her.

But when, after Flo's second warning that it was now 8.45 and only fifteen minutes until my breakfast would be ready, I went along the verandah I found my friend, hollow-eyed from a sleepless night, sitting on her two-foot-six bed, poring over a time-table. . . .

The thought of sleeping in our own beds that night so cheered us that breakfasting with a thousand other campers, who could not forbear to cheer whenever a waitress dropped a piece of cutlery, and who gave a full-throated response, 'Bye-bye', two strongly enunciated words, to the Redcoat's 'Bye-bye', at the end of his announcement of the day's gaieties, could not quench in us the feeling that all was sweetness and light. When for about the third or fourth time the Awful Child next to her leaned across Kathleen's plate, the sleeve of his jacket dipping in her tea, as he reached for yet another slab of white sliced bread, she turned upon him a benign smile.

We tried to leave the camp by the gate by which we had returned to it after an escape into the town the night before, but it was padlocked. We wandered about following various signs which said To the Sea, To the Esplanade, but which always brought us up against the meshed-wire fencing which encloses the camp. We were beginning to feel claustrophobic when we came upon a workman to whom we explained our dilemma— 'We want to get out!'—and who unpadlocked a gate for us and other escapees. There was a great sense of freedom in tramping along the unenclosed sand, beside the unbounded sea.

Somewhere near the pier we went up to the promenade and made our way to the Town Centre. We found the 'bus station, and there was a 'bus leaving in a few minutes for Chichester. Sometimes, though not often, life is on one's side.

The scenery was nothing much, but the fields and hedges

were green with young spring, there was blossom everywhere, and the first lilac and the last narcissi, and in the near distance the South Downs flowed down gently to the coastal plain. Butlin's, with its garish plastic flowers, its 'grotto' full of tartish-looking pink plastic mermaids, its vast, hot, airless halls, milling with people and deafening with the hollow sound of loudly relayed canned pop music, retreated into a dim memory of a bad dream. Reality was the quiet green countryside, the gardens of wallflowers and tulips rising from mists of forget-me-nots.

We came soon to the outskirts of the city; the cathedral spire came into view, and at the end of a street there was a glimpse of the beautiful sixteenth-century market-cross, octagonal and or-nately carved. We alighted from the 'bus beside the cathedral, and my heart sang as when I stepped out of the railway station and saw the walls of York, for this was beauty of the same great order, but Norman, not Roman. This noble church was built by Bishop Ralph Luffa, in the twelfth century, in the reign of William Rufus, but after damage by fire was restored in the thirteenth, when new and Gothic features were intro-duced. The high altar is a mixture of Gothic and Norman—and twentieth century, for in 1966 the Friends of the Cathedral gave a panelled tapestry, designed by John Piper and woven by Pinton Frères, of Aubusson, France.

According to a printed statement left for the visitor on the altar rail this tapestry 'symbolises God in His Three Persons, in the heart of His creation'. The symbols of the evangelists, from the Book of Revelation, are realistic, but the rest is highly ab-stract, and whilst I had no difficulty with Piper's work at Coventry—indeed, nothing but admiration—I found this difficult in its abstractions, and its colours too violent. A man standing near me observed to his companion that it was 'violent and crude'. Violent, certainly, but not, I think, crude, for a very great deal of religous imaginativeness has gone, obviously, into its creation. It would have belonged more easily, I felt, in

Coventry than in this ancient, traditional setting. Graham Sutherland is represented here, too, with a painting (1961) of the Risen Christ with St. Mary Magdalene, in the chapel of St. Mary Magdalene, behind the high altar.

There has been controversy about the restoration of the ornate 'Arundel Screen' at the west end of the choir; this was removed in 1860 and stored in the bell tower, which is separate from the cathedral, but replaced in 1961 as a memorial to Bishop George Bell (1929–58). Those who deplore the restoration of the screen contend that it shuts off the choir from the body of the church, which of course it does; but those who defend its restoration do so on the ground that the choir is a 'church within a church', in which the community gather as a family for worship, and that the atmosphere of corporate worship was weakened when the screen was removed. I would personally always dispense with screens, on purely aesthetic grounds; I like an unobstructed view through the choir to the glory of the east window.

The tomb of Bishop Luffa (1091–1123) is a dark marble 'coffin' in the south transept, placed on the ground beside the wall, so modest an affair that it would be easy to overlook it. I liked some light, plain-glass windows here inset with stained glass figures of such distinguished personalities as Charles Marriott, first principal of the Chichester Theological College, who died in 1858; John Lake, Bishop of Chichester (one of the Seven Bishops), 1685–9; Oliver Whitby, founder of the school that bears his name, who died in 1702. I liked, also, the tomb of Richard Fitz Alan, Earl of Arundel, and his countess, 1346–97; and was interested in a chapel 'extended and beautified' by Gilbert Sancto Leofardo, bishop, 1278–1305, and restored 'in affectionate memory of Ashurst Turner Gilbert, bishop, 1842–70'.

What I did not like was the restoration to the top of the fifteenth-century bell tower, which seemed to me incredibly crude. The fifteenth-century spire of the cathedral was restored by Sir Gilbert Scott, after it suddenly crashed at 1.30 p.m. on February 21, 1861. The restoration took six years and is an amazing piece of work. The spire is 277 feet high and can be seen out to sea.

At the end of a short turning facing the bell tower there is a small cobbled square, flanked by old houses, St. Martin's Square, and here is the doorway to the covered entrance to Chichester's famous almshouses, the Hospital of the Blessed Mary, popularly known as St. Mary's Hospital, which at this present site dates from the thirteenth century. The door of the porter's cottage is on the left in the archway upon which the door in the wall opens. The Hospital—which, of course, it no longer is—is a strange-looking building a few yards across a small garden. Its immensely high and steep red-tiled roof is to be glimpsed above high walls as you walk along the street, and if you do not know what it is you are hard put to it to say, for it could be some kind of chapel, you feel, with its square turret, or it could be a very fine old private house, or an old Quaker meeting-house. It is very remarkable, and it is very beautiful.

It is, in fact, both chapel and dwelling-house, for under that forty-five-foot-high steep roof there is a great raftered hall, the east end of which is a chapel, with a beautiful window of plain glass, in the Early Decorated style, inset with a stained glass figure of the Virgin and Child. The chapel occupies about a third of the great hall, and is divided from the dwelling part by a carved oak screen which is probably the oldest in England in its original state. The dwelling part, which consists of eight little almshouses, is in turn separated from the broad nave by wooden railings which screen off tiny kitchens, each with a sink, electric cooker, and small refrigerator. A door leads into a small sitting-room, with a bedroom opening out; these rooms look out through latticed windows under the steep roof on to a garden of grass and flower borders and fruit trees, all very pleasantly laid out and of great old-world charm. A door in the kitchen enclosure leads into a small but modernly equipped bathroom. The rooms are centrally heated, and home-help is available, and it was to be observed that all the tiny kitchens were spotlessly clean.

The porter's wife, who showed us over the place, knocked on one of the doors and an elderly woman readily agreed to let us see her little home. We were admitted to a comfortable, homely room full of photographs and knicknacks, and when we remarked on how cosy it was its owner smiled and agreed, adding, 'and we're all quite free. We're as free as you are!' She was anxious, I think, to have us understand that an almshouse was a private home like any other, not part of an institution. The residents pay no rent, nor do they pay for light or heating, and they receive six shillings a week in alms, in addition to their State pension and any supplementary assistance they may receive. In the old days, in addition to their weekly alms' allowance they were given ten shillings a week every two years, 'in lieu of a new gown'. It was intended that three of the cottages should be for married couples, but in recent years these have not been found in the Welfare State, and at present all eight cottages are occupied singly by women.

The place was founded in the thirteenth century for the aged and sick, with beds along each side of the nave, and homeless people were received late at night and given shelter. It was laid down in the regulations that these people must 'go forth early in the morning', and on arrival must have their feet washed; they were required not to annoy the sick, nor to pilfer, and to 'behave respectfully in word and deed'. And the sexes were to be separated. Anyone found to be deceiving the Warden as to his means was to have the money he sought to conceal hung round his neck and to be 'well flogged and do penance for thirty days'.

Today, all that is required of the alms people is that they shall attend a short service in the chapel five mornings a week; there is no service on Saturdays, and on Sunday they are free to attend places of worship of their choice.

At the Reformation the character of the hospital changed; it ceased to be an infirmary, and although the sick and 'casuals' were still helped to some extent the place became a house of rest 'for five poor brethren and sisters'. In 1660 the use of the hall as an infirmary was entirely discontinued; the beds were taken away and the present eight small two-roomed cottages were created—the kitchens are a modern innovation. In 1680 four tall chimneys were built to serve the fireplaces in the eight cottages. At the time, this necessary addition to the building gave rise to controversy, and Archbishop H. P. Wright, in his book, *The Story of the 'Domus Dei' of Chichester*, demanded: 'Clear out everything that uglifies the finely-proportioned Hall, not forgetting the hideous chimneys, rising repulsively and penetrating the sloped roof, a barbarous attack upon brilliant mediaeval architecture.' I doubt whether anyone today would find the red brick chimneys unaesthetic, though with oil-fired central heating and electric cookers and fires they are no longer necessary. When the central heating was installed in 1965 the coal bunker for each flat was removed and the space utilised for bathrooms.

Apart from the general impressiveness of the great raftered fourteenth-century hall, and the uniqueness of the little alms-houses built into it, the chapel itself is of interest. The wooden screen is a fine example of medieval carving, and is in intact, and there are some remarkably carved misericords depicting strange creatures—a merman, and a harpy, a beautiful woman with an evil vulture body, to mention two that stay in the memory. According to the late Canon A. G. Powell, a former Custos of St. Mary's,[1] so closely do these misericords resemble, 'in technique and queer imagination, the misericords in the Cathedral

1. In a booklet published in 1966, *The Hospital of the Blessed Mary, Chichester*, available at the hospital.

choir that may well have come from the same workshop. The are certainly of a similar date.'

Nobody knows when the original east window fell into ruin, for the aperture was blocked up by broken bits of stone and rubble until 1880, when it was decided to remake the window using such scraps of the old stone tracery as were usable, filling in the gaps with new stone, and as far as possible reproducing the original window. It was this nineteenth-century recon-struction which was destroyed by bomb blast in 1943. The existing window was made in 1950, with the beautiful central panel of the Virgin and Child designed by Christopher Webb, whose similar work—plain glass with coloured centre panels—appears also in the cathedral, as we have seen.

We retraced our steps to the Market Cross, which is the finest of its kind in the country, and crossing one of the four roads which converge on it, found our way by a homing in-stinct to one of Chichester's numerous old-world pubs, where, in a reaction against Butlin's, we drank good sherry and honest stout, and ate fresh green salads. Kathleen, at breakfast, had ordered a grilled kipper and had been 'greatly astonied', as it says in the Bible, at being served with four little brown fillets that bore no resemblance to the delicious crisply grilled heart-shaped fish of her imagining. The little brown slivers had no doubt been part of a kippered herring at one time, but between that time and their appearance on a plate in Butlin's there had been in carceration in a packet in the tomb of a deep-freeze . . . I, who reckon to breakfast off a piece of toast and China tea, had pulled the cotton-wool inside out of a white roll and smeared the husk with a popular brand of marmalade, taken a sip of the Indian tea in a metal pot, and hoped for better things in Chichester. The green salad, with Cheddar cheese grated over it, was very welcome. (In fairness to Butlin's it should be said that if you do not want Indian tea out of a metal pot you can have instant coffee out of a metal pot. The cups are—of course—plastic.)

Fortified by this pleasant break we set off to look at the Palants, four streets, north, south, east and west, which were part of the palatinate of the Archbishop of Canterbury. These narrow streets are handsome with seventeenth- and eighteenth-century houses and cottages; some are small and half-timbered, others stately with yellow façades and deep windows, in the Wren manner. One, in West Street, is in fact attributed to Sir Christopher Wren. It is very pleasant to stroll along these narrow streets, admiring the houses of different periods, and it is satisfactory on leaving the Pallants to come suddenly upon a terrace of houses and not know whether they are old houses skilfully restored, or new houses built in a manner befitting this fine old city.

Chichester has a thirteenth-century Guildhall, formerly a Grey Friar's chapel, and a church, St. Olave's, in the construction of which Roman materials were used. It also has remains of the Roman walls, a mile and a half of them, known as the North Walls. As walls they they are unexciting and bear no comparison with those of York and Chester; a few steps up a grassy bank brings you to a broad path and a low parapet; there is no feeling of height and nothing to indicate the Roman fortifications, though these remains of the walls follow their line; they offer, merely, a pleasant walk to the north of the city.

We got back to Butlin's too early for the high-tea at six-thirty, and went and looked at the indoor swimming-pool, on an upper floor, and roofed over with a jungle of plastic tropical foliage and flowers from which plastic parrots are suspended. Down below, beside the mermaids' grotto, this swimming-pool becomes a huge tank with a glass side, lit in such a way that the bodies of the swimmers are visible; the effect is very odd—disconcerting. The adjoining mermaids' grotto is also contained in glass, and cunningly lit; but beyond these illuminated tanks is a semi-darkness, rows of chairs, and television.

It would be pleasant, we think, leaving the swimming-pool, to sit in a bar and have a drink before the evening meal, but the bars are huge hot noisy halls, with bar-counters half a mile long. We settled for cups of tea from a self-service snack-bar at one end of the hall below the swimming-pool; it, too, is hot and noisy; we sit as close to the exit as possible in order to get the air let in when it swings to and fro from the endless in-and-out of happy campers. I ask the elderly woman at the cash-desk how she can sit there all day long in that heat and noise; she looks surprised and says, 'Oh, you get used to it. You never notice it.'

On the way back to the 'chalet lines' I notice that at the ends of the lanes the gables of each motel-like terrace of chalets offer a 'Bavarian' façade, with wooden shutters. We lie on our beds until the dulcet voice of 'Flo' trickles in through the public-address system over the door, preceded by some treacly music, saying she would like to remind us that 'your evening meal will be ready at six-thirty'.

Shortly before six-thirty there is the tramp of people along the verandahs and down below in the lane, people knocking on each other's doors, calling to each other, and soon there is a steady flow, a mass movement, towards the huge hall, where, a thousand strong and eight to a table, rubbing shoulders, we shall sit down to dine. There are so many of us we have to queue up to get in. Once inside the service is prompt. Soup is poured from jugs and the high-piled plates of slabs of white bread are passed to and fro. Some break their bread up into the soup. Soon the waitresses are tippeting down the aisles with what look like old-fashioned tiered cake-stands; on each tier is a plate of food, each plate identical. On the plate this evening there is a slice of tinned meat of some kind warmed up with a slice of warmed tinned pineapple; there is a small heap of tinned peas, and a heap of fried potatoes. I taste the square of meat out of curiosity, but cannot determine what it is; some kind of luncheon meat, perhaps? This is followed by a portion of brown steamed pudding sitting in a watery custard. We ask if we might have cheese instead, and the waitress brings us each a cube of cellophane-wrapped cheese ice-cold from a freeze, and some biscuits. The Awful Child complains about the custard, and is once again rebuked for reaching across the lady's plate, this time for the sugar castor. But liberation is at hand, and again the lady smiles sweetly.

Seated at the end of the table we are able to leave without disturbing anyone. The girl on my left, big sister to the Awful Child, is dolled up in orange and yellow nylon, cut low at the back, and hung with bright green beads, with ear-rings to match; and there are other signs of dressiness around; Saturday night is the big night. What a flinging around of dustbins there will be in the chalet lines tonight! A wicked parody of a lovely Ralph Hodgson poem comes into my mind:

> Picture the lewd delight
> Deep in the lines tonight!
> 'Butlin's!' the cry goes round,
> 'Butlin's again!'

The previous evening we had humped our bags, growing heavier and heavier, up and down the chalet lines for half an hour searching for our chalets, which no one had told us were on the upper level, until we were almost in tears from frustration and despair. This evening we were lucky enough to find a trolley someone had parked in a corner and we set off for the reception hall almost at a canter. It was, of course, empty, its vast open spaces untenanted; behind the long counter a young man sat looking very bored, and an elderly woman stood expressionless. They regarded us purely blankly as we approached. I said we had come to hand in our keys as we were leaving. The woman took the keys and refunded the half-crown deposited on each. She came to life to ask was there any special reason why we were leaving.

'No,' I said, 'no special reason. Only that we haven't liked it very much. . . .'

Perhaps no one had ever said anything so monstrous to her before, for the explanation seemed to strike her dumb. Perhaps it really was preposterous on our parts. There's a Butlin leaflet which proudly declares, 'A million people can't be wrong!'

Something fallacious about that. But leaving aside the political illustrations of the fallacy which spring to mind let us say, simply, that tastes differ, and one man's meat, etc. Certainly our fellow-campers at that special 'reunion weekend' were having a high old time. That is what was so frightening.

II

Ely, via Cambridge

HAVING since my childhood a predilection for rebels, outlaws, and outsiders in general, Hereward the Wake always seemed to me one of the great romantic characters of English history. I liked to think of him and his men bobbing up among the reeds in the Fens to draw a bow at the Norman conquerors. All my life I thought of the Fens like that, miles and miles of marshland, dense jungles of reeds, with here and there passage-ways cut through them for flat-bottom boats, like the marshes in the south of Iraq, and the great bog in the south of Brittany, near St. Nazaire, the Grande Brière. I explored the Grande Brière in the fifties, when I was writing a book about Brittany;[1] it proved to be not as watery as I had expected, the houses were not islanded like the villages of the marsh Arabs of Iraq, but it was marshland, with dykes and ditches and causeways, and here and there watery lanes. Our English Fens must be like that, I thought, with the Isle of Ely a ridge in the midst of it all, crowned by the cathedral, and everything, even perhaps the cathedral, looking very much as in the days of Hereward the Wake. It must be, I thought, a completely fascinating place. I did no reading on the subject, and it did not occur to anyone to tell me that the Fens were drained ages ago, through successive centuries, and converted into cultivable land. It was something

1. *Country of the Sea*, 1957.

everyone knew, even if they didn't know exactly when; everyone except me, apparently, still bogged down—and bogged is the word—in the romantic notion.

I was still an innocent in this matter the day I set out with Gilbert Turner to drive through darkest Middlesex to Cambridge, en route for Ely. Gilbert's observation that if it rained when we went to the Fens it wouldn't matter, as it would only make them look 'fennier', merely confirmed me in the romantic illusion. In point of fact it didn't rain that cold grey day in early May, though later it snowed.

The industrialised wilderness of Willesden and Hendon was new to me, and the Brent flyover, flyover over flyover, startled me because I had seen nothing like it since I was in Chicago the previous year. But at Mill Hill the greyness yielded to the bright spring green of trees and hedges, with outbreaks of ornamental cherry-blossom, and the Great North Road took on beauty, plunging on through green and wooded country, and at one stretch flanked by tall poplars, like a French road.

At Hatfield there were blossom-trees and grass verges; the road narrows here, but is being widened. Soon afterwards Ayot St. Lawrence, George Bernard Shaw's last home, is three miles off to the left, in pleasant rural country. There are a good many heavy lorries, and though the new town of Stevenage is by-passed there are factories again, and tall blocks of flats.

The pleasant old village of Graveley now has the Great North Road running through it, but its peace will be restored, I gather, when the Baldock by-pass is opened.

Suddenly the country opens out to a wide vista across the green Midlands Plain to a blue horizon, and the road narrows to become a country road with hawthorn hedges topping grassy banks, and soon the little town of Baldock is reached, with trees in the wide main street, and Queen Anne and Georgian houses, and some even older, seventeenth century, timbered, with overhanging upper storeys.

We leave the Great North Road here and head due east for

Cambridge. Now there are wide open cornlands, without hedges, and the land is gently undulating. It is still Hertfordshire, but at Royston we reach the border, and at Melbourn we are among the thatched-roofed cottages of Cambridgeshire. Soon after that we are in the wooded suburbs of the university city of Cambridge. I put away my notebook and allow pure enchantment to take over. Perhaps that does not make for good reportage, but beauty is notoriously difficult to report factually.

It was so grey a day, and the wind so cold, yet I kept pausing to look back, to look again, and all the time exclaiming helplessly, 'It's so beautiful! I'd forgotten how beautiful Cambridge is!' I doubt if anywhere else in England is so much architectural beauty crowded into one place. We walked across a broad green open space called Parker's Piece, the grass almost too good to walk on, and came into a crowded narrow main street, and almost immediately were looking across more wonderful lawn to Emmanuel College, with Sir Christopher Wren's noble loggia reminding me of Greenwich. Behind lies a classical chapel, also designed by Wren.

Almost next door is Christ's College, and here are handsome buildings built round a quadrangle of striped lawn, and under the sixteenth-century—and earlier—walls are wallflowers and tulips rising from mists of forget-me-not, and below an oriel window the lion and the unicorn, the arms of the foundress, Lady Margaret Beaufort, mother of Henry VII. There are some mediaeval stone-framed windows here; there has been, apparently, a good deal of restoration, some buildings restored almost out of recognition, yet it is still so beautiful, so very beautiful, and I find myself wondering whether the students strolling along the paths at the edge of the lawns, some of them long-haired and wearing jeans, with the conventional contemporary scruffiness, realise how fortunate they are to be studying in so beautiful a place; whether, even, they are aware of its beauty.

We cross the road and cut through a little narrow street called
Petty Cury, and past the open-air market square, and across
another road, and come to a huge and splendid area of vast
lawn with important-looking statuary in the middle and a group
of buildings with towers and pinnacles, most wonderful to
behold, and part of it like some great cathedral. I exclaim upon
its beauty and ask what it is, and am told, 'King's College
Chapel.' The tone is mildly surprised; there are things one is
supposed to know, but though I have been in Cambridge
before I did not know: it had to wait till now, so late in the
day, and I am glad, for in youth one takes so much for granted.
The interior of King's College Chapel, Cambridge, is perhaps
best described as a vast hall of Tudor stone exquisitely carved
into a kind of lace work, fanning out into a series of arches in
the immensely high vaulted ceiling, and all enclosed by huge
windows of rich coloured glass. The east, south and north
windows were created between 1515 and 1531; the west
window is Victorian. The windows depict Biblical scenes, and
the deep crimson, gold and blue of the sixteenth-century glass is
almost indescribable in its richness.

There is no electricity in the chapel; it is lit by white candles
contained in plain glass shades, ranged along the stalls. I have
been told, and can well imagine, that evensong in the chapel,
with all the candles lit, and the famous King's College Chapel
Choir singing, is a profoundly moving experience.

(There is similarly no electricity installed in the art gallery of
the Fitzwilliam Museum, in Trumpington Street, south of the
City Centre, a handsome mid-nineteenth-century building with
a classical pillared entrance which houses the great collection of
paintings, books, illuminated manuscripts, which Richard,
7th Viscount Fitzwilliam, bequeathed to the university in
1816, along with £100,000 for the construction of a building
to house the collection. The Fitzwilliam Museum was built in
1835, to the design of George Basevi, the winner of a competition in which there were twenty-seven entries. In the winter

the art gallery closes earlier and earlier, as the daylight fades.)

There are a few historic facts about the chapel which are of interest: King's College was founded by that pious but unfortunate king, Henry VI, and he laid the foundation stone of the chapel in July, 1445, but it was not completed until the reign of Henry VIII. The organ screen, a magnificent example of Italian work, was erected when Anne Boleyn was queen.

Beyond the green sward before the west front of the chapel a little grey stone bridge, the King's Bridge, crosses the narrow river, overhung by willows trailing to the water. Nearby, to the right, across the grass, a wrought-iron gate leads into a lovely garden, extending a little distance along the Backs—the famous riverside walk which looks across to the backs of colleges and their landscaped gardens. This garden, then, was full of wallflowers, tulips, blossoming trees, with phlox and lupins and delphiniums waiting in the wings for the spring ballet to be over and the curtain rung up on the summer. Beautiful at all seasons, Cambridge must be, even in winter, when the architecture of bare trees adds its own harmony to that of grey stone and red brick.

The old part of St. John's, founded by Lady Margaret Beaufort in 1509, and which is all of brick, has been cleaned and looks, now, astonishingly new. The massive gateway, with towers at each side, is very impressive; above the entrance arch Lady Margaret Beaufort's arms are nobly carved in stone. The New Buildings of St. John's are early nineteenth century, and handsome in their Gothic Revival fashion. Jesus College also has a tower gateway, square, red brick, Tudor Gothic, completed at the beginning of the sixteenth century, and the great gate of Trinity College, built in 1518, was decorated a hundred years later by the figures of James I and his wife and son to commemorate their visit. Trinity is the largest of the colleges, with cloisters and an early seventeenth-century fountain.

There were other colleges, but I have remembered them only as a series of handsome buildings, noble gateways, incredible lawns, borders of wallflowers and tulips. Only one thing more stands out clearly, and that is the small round Church of the Holy Sepulchre, dating from the twelfth century, but so ruthlessly restored in the mid-nineteenth that very little of the original fabric remains. But it is unique as the oldest of the four remaining round churches in England. Inside, if you drop a sixpence into a box and turn a switch, the dome is floodlit for a minute or two. The church stands on Bridge Street, and you come to it from St. John's College, across the lovely cloistered Bridge of Sighs which spans the river and connects the old buildings with the new.

There are other churches of importance to see: Great St. Mary's, the University Church, begun in 1478, but not completed—from lack of money—until the seventeenth; and the Church of St. Benedict, known as St. Bene't's, part of which is the oldest building in Cambridge, being late Saxon. But after the Round Church I was incapable of taking any more in . . . and it was beginning to sleet; it seemed better to turn in under the high grey wall bounding Jesus Lane and head back for Parker's Piece and the road for the Isle of Ely.

All is flat and green, with grazing black and white cows and nothing of any interest. The moment of disenchantment is at hand for when I remark on the dullness of the landscape my companion murmurs, 'Well, of course, the Fens . . .'

'These are the Fens—these flat fields?'

'They were drained, you know . . .'

I hadn't known, of course; that was my trouble. I gaze bleakly—almost tearfully—at the dull good pastureland that was once a romantic hideout for Hereward the Wake. It was a very long time ago, to be sure, going on for nine hundred years, and at least the Fens haven't been 'developed', that sinister contemporary word, or taken over by the War Office and ominously placarded with Keep Out signs; at least they are still green and criss-crossed with dykes; drained and converted

K

to pastureland they are still fens. This I can accept, once the first shock of disappointment is past, and that the Isle of Ely is, by the same token, no longer an island. But that the cathedral should not stand out on a ridge, visible from afar in the low-lying land—this is the final blow to the romantic illusion. It does, of course, stand out in the sense that you see its high castellated tower for some time before you see the first houses of the small market town which is the city of Ely, but the 'Isle', the highest point in the Fens, on which the cathedral stands, is a hillock rising only 120 feet on the west bank of the Ouse, an upland seven miles long and four miles wide.

But suddenly, however you have imagined it, the reality of it is there, golden in the fenland greenness, dominating the scene, and when you come close, revealing an almost unimaginable and indescribable beauty. The precincts are beautiful with grass and trees and mediaeval houses and other buildings. They are centuries later than the cathedral, but that they should have grown up round it, in a harmony of red brick, grey stone, mullioned windows, seems somehow right. The great gateway to the abbey, now a school for boys, was built in 1394. Close to it is a steep-roofed chapel, Crauden's Chapel, built by Alan of Walsingham in 1324 for the use of Prior Crauden; it has been described as 'one of the most curious and valuable Decorated remains in the country'.

There is a good deal of historic interest in the precincts of the cathedral, but with that tremendous Norman edifice towering above everything else it is not easy to take it in. One is only confusedly aware of a wealth of beautiful old red roofs, stone-framed windows, old walls. The history of the cathedral is long and complicated, but, briefly, it began with the abbey founded by St. Etheldreda, wife of King Egfrid, 'King of the East English', in 673. It was sacked by the Danes in 870, and re-founded by the Benedictines in 970. It remained a Benedictine monastery until the reign of Henry VIII, when, with the dissolution of the monasteries, it became a cathedral.

The great Norman church which survived the centuries to become a cathedral still standing in the late twentieth century goes back to a Norman monk, the Abbot Simeon, who was given charge of the monastery by William the Conqueror. Simeon considered the Anglo-Saxon edifice not good enough, and the great Norman church which forms the greater part of the cathedral as we know it today was begun in 1080.

The cathedral is entered by the west door, known as the Galilee Porch; which is early thirteenth century and extremely beautiful, being intricately carved, and set in the most exqusite carved stone work. From this porch one looks down the great length of the cathedral to the east window, a distance of 537 feet. The vista is one of immensely high Norman columns rising with an astonishing grace to the painted wooden ceiling. That the nave is empty of pews adds to the immensity.

When you reach the choir screen you come to something unique and wonderful—the Octagon, where eight walls with arches and stained-glass windows support an enormous circular glass tower in the roof—the great lantern constructed early in the fourteenth century after the Norman tower of the Abbot Simeon crashed. The idea of the lantern was Alan of Walsingham's, and the man who carried out his design was Edward III's carpenter, William Hurley. It is a masterpiece of mediaeval engineering and craftsmanship, and I would use the word miracle in connection with it, because the lantern was constructed of eight oak beams, uprights of sixty-three feet, rising from timbers which had to support 400 tons of wood and lead—and did, and do. By what means were they hauled into position? It would be a major engineering feat even today, but the work was carried out over 600 years ago. Well, they did it, and it's still there, and it's only possible to gaze up at it and marvel. There is some astonishingly beautiful painting up there in the lantern roof, and the light filters down from the clear glass of the lantern into the ornate mediaeval beauty of the Octagon.

There is everywhere in the cathedral a wealth of ornate wood and stone carving beyond my power to describe, though mention must be made of scenes from the life of St. Etheldreda marvellously carved in stone on the pillars of the Octagon, and the grotesque but fascinating carvings on the miserere seats in the choir—where the services in the cathedral are now held, and which is candle-lit like King's College Chapel.

The Lady Chapel is huge, and separate from the main body of the cathedral. It was begun in 1321, when the Norman tower collapsed, and was finished in 1349. It is attributed to a monk, John Wisbech, working under Alan of Walsingham. It was used as a parish church from 1566 until as late as 1938, when it reverted to its original purpose. It was the last work undertaken by the monastery, and is considered a triumph both of architecture and sculpture. It is full of delicately beautiful stone carving, and contained innumerable small stone statues, including a series depicting the life of the Virgin, but during the Reformation all were relentlessly attacked, and in every instance the head has been smashed by a hammer, and only small particles of the original stained glass remain in the great windows. At the east end there are on the walls traces of the bright colours which originally characterised the whole building. In the cathedral itself there are similar traces, together with some modern restoration—which does not, somehow, seem a good idea, presenting, now, an artificial appearance.

A mistake, too, seems the modern sculpture—not dated—by David Wynne, of Christ and Mary Magdalene in the north transept. Christ is depicted in a short shirt and Mary in a short tight dress, her hands raised. The sculpture is in green bronze and is grotesque in the modern manner. It is highly contemporary. Perhaps it has something to 'say' to the younger generation of today; certainly modern art has to find a place in our ancient cathedrals if they are to be, as Milton said of books, not absolutely dead things but contain a potency of life in them. Down through history each century has made its contributions to our great churches, and the twentieth century has its contributions to make; it is just a pity that the art of the late twentieth century is so often harsh, violent, a travesty of life . . . though perhaps that harshness and violence, that grotesquerie, does in fact interpret our times. It could be, alas. For me the modern sculpture in Ely Cathedral struck as discordant a note as the John Piper altar tapestry, in its violent colours, in that other Norman cathedral, Chichester. But I would not have liked the David Wynne sculpture even in the modern setting of Coventry, where I liked so much that was entirely contemporary in spirit.

We decided to have some tea before starting on the long drive back to London. We went into a hotel and ordered tea and toast; after a long wait a waitress brought a tray on which there was only tea, and a bill stating tea-and-toast five shillings. The request for toast being repeated, after another long wait she returned with it, then altered the bill to seven-and-six. When it was pointed out that the bill stated tea-and-toast five shillings she said, in the weary, bored tone English waitresses commonly use to customers, 'With toast it's another two-and-six.' Ah, the English, the English! Our policemen may no longer be so wonderful, but our waitresses certainly are.

The English climate is wonderful, too, because later, in Hertfordshire, on that day in the sweet month of May, we found the fields white with snow.

12

Norwich, the Provincial Capital

FOR years I had been hearing from an old friend about a church in Norwich he always referred to as the 'wistaria church'. Invariably in May, when the wistaria was in bloom at the back of my house, he would say, 'I wish you would one day go to Norwich and see the wistaria church!'

So that when I came to plan this book and decided that Norwich was an old city I would like to include it was natural to inquire of my friend the name and whereabouts of his 'wistaria church'.

The name he had forgotten, 'but anyone would tell you— just ask for the church with the wistaria trees. It's up a steep hill from the market place and on the way to the big Catholic church. . . .'

As a direction it seemed on a level with the all-too-familiar one, 'Get off the 'bus at the cinema, and then it's just in behind,' with the inevitable rider, 'You can't miss it!' Which of course one easily can. But Norwich, I was to discover, is a city in which it is very easy to find your way about; it is compact, and it is well signposted. When you emerge from Thorpe Station the main road leads directly to the castle, which is approximately at the City Centre. A bridge crosses the narrow River Wensum, where a number of yachts and motor-boats and other small craft are tied up; at one side of the bridge, where the boats are, the river is attractive, with trees; on the other side, where it is wider, it is singularly dreary; the river half encircles the city, east and north, and, as at York, in places meets the city walls, stretches of which remain, south-east, and to the west.

The main road, the Prince of Wales Road, with its red buses, and a pursuing smell of the British national dish, fish-and-chips, climbs up past the General Post Office to the low grassy mound on which the castle stands, and sweeping round becomes Castle Meadow. All that remains of the castle, founded at the time of the Conquest, is the massive square stone keep; it is early twelfth century, but was re-faced in the nineteenth; it is ornate, with four tiers of arcading, and much more suggestive of the nineteenth century than the twelfth . . . though the interior is grey stone and starkly Norman, with battlements and dungeons which may be visited at stated times and upon the payment of two shillings.

The castle is now a museum of art, local archaeology and natural history; there is a Norfolk Room with stuffed birds and animals in their characteristic East Anglian settings; there are Romano-British relics, and in the Colman Galleries (Colman, the mustard) a huge collection of the paintings of John Sell Cotman and John Crome, the most celebrated of the Norwich School of painters, and of their contemporaries and successors; but gazing, a little dazedly, down these long galleries I had the feeling of it being Cotman all the way . . . until suddenly I walked into a small room and was confronted by the horrifying works of one of our leading contemporary painters, Francis Bacon. In the lovely gardens of the Castle Hill, where the lilac and azaleas were in bloom, and the last tulips lingered among the crimson and golden wallflowers, an exhibition of modern outdoor sculpture had been assembled on the grass, grotesque shapes, obscure abstractions, and something which looked like yellow plastic intestines. Norwich, it would seem, is determined to be 'with it'.

The art galleries and the museum are on the ground floor of

the keep; in the centre there are glass cases with displays of Lowestoft china, Norwich silver and local antiquities. A gallery now runs round the first-floor level, the floor having been removed. There are arches of a later period, yellow against the sombre grey stone of the Norman walls, and there is an ancient well, quite frighteningly deep. There was a civic reception the day I was there, and the red carpet, potted hydrangeas and ferns, and teacups laid out on long trestle tables, seemed strangely at odds with the twelfth-century setting, like a party in a dungeon.

Outside, there was the strong sweet smell of the cow-parsley which covered the castle mound; the mound is artificial, and not high, but it offers a good view out over the city, on all sides. On the eastern side you look down on to what was the cattle market but which is now a car park; at the other side you look across Castle Meadow to the market place, the civic centre, with the old Guildhall to the right and the modern City Hall rising behind, From Castle Meadow a narrow passage, with some steps, Davey Place, brings you to the market place, with its gay multi-coloured roofs. To the left of the market place is the great parish church of St. Peter Mancroft, built in the mid-fifteenth century by the wealthy wool merchants of the city to serve the Mancroft ward, the rich central ward of the city, the civic centre; the name is a corruption of Manne's Croft. The interior of the church is lofty and noble; the richly coloured glass of the east window is of the fifteenth and sixteenth centuries, and depicts some of the merchants, in their magnificent robes; it is the work of local craftsmen.

Beside the church, in a railed-off enclosure, is a statue of Sir Thomas Browne, who is buried in the church. From my youth up I had admired the author of *Religio Medici*, but had not known that he had practised in Norwich as a physician for the greater part of his life, was knighted there by Charles II in 1671, and died there in 1682 on his seventy-seventh birthday. The statue was erected, off the narrow Haymarket, in October 1903, and says that he was for many years resident near that spot. His house, however, which John Evelyn described as a 'paradise and cabinet of rarities', disappeared long ago.

The market place is the site of the Norman settlement, which had been selected as a convenient area, being free of Saxons, and protected by the castle overlooking it. Today it is a settlement of some two hundred well stocked stalls with fruit, vegetables, flowers, and small shops selling delicatessen goods, poultry, meat, cakes; there are also snack-bars selling soft drinks, and, judging by smells emanating from them, hot-dogs and chips; all is roofed over with the red and blue and white and yellow awnings, the effect of which, from a distance, is of a patch-work quilt.

The Guildhall is small and grey and fifteenth century, but like the castle had a face-lift in the nineteenth, when it was 'much altered'. It is open free to the public in the afternoons, except when it is in use. The Council Hall is much as it was in the sixteenth century; it has an interesting carved ceiling, a big church-like window with some old glass, and Tudor portraits on panelled walls.

The new City Hall was opened by George VI in 1938, and Norwich claims that it is the finest modern town hall in the country. It is of brick, with a pillared porch and a tall square clock tower, a brick campanile rising high above the ornate little grey Guildhall, and starkly twentieth century by comparison, yet very nobly and handsomely dominating the scene so that it is the fussiness of the Guildhall which, if anything, does not belong.

The shopping thoroughfare skirting the market place is less distinguished than its name, which is Gentlemen's Walk; at one end of it is the Haymarket and the Mancroft Church, and at the other the Guildhall. If you cross the market place at the top, in front of the City Hall, and turn up the hill into Giles' Street, with the Guildhall below, you come to the wistaria church, properly called St. Giles-on-the-Hill, but sure enough ringed round most charmingly with little wistaria trees. According to the Official Guide St. Giles' Street is the 'best remaining Georgian street in the city, though much gapped with Victorian buildings and cut about by modern shop fronts. From the time of Sir Thomas Browne onwards Norwich has been the home of celebrated doctors, and St. Giles' in the eighteenth and nineteenth centuries was the local Harley Street.' That the office of the Medical Officer of Health is housed at Churchman House, perhaps the finest of the old houses in the area, in a sense maintains the medical tradition.

The church, in its present form, is fourteenth century and its Perpendicular tower is reputedly the highest of the city churches. I did not find the church—which is High Anglican—of much interest or beauty, either inside or out; but it is finely sited, at the top of the hill, surrounded by old houses which at one side give almost the effect of a cathedral close.

A short distance further on there is the massive Gothic Revival Roman Catholic church of St. John the Baptist; it was built by the fifteenth Duke of Norfolk, the father of the present duke, in 1884, and completed in 1910. It is cathedral-vast, with a square central tower and a number of small towers dotted Gothically about. So far as I am concerned it is completely hideous, but those who defend it use the word 'imposing' in connection with it, and point out that it is built of good honest stone, which is unusual in modern Gothic. At which point I mutter, *sotto voce:* 'So is Guildford, and with more grace.'

Opposite there is a synagogue, and if you continue on down Earlham Road you come to the beautiful seventeenth century mansion of Earlham Hall, housing the offices of the new University of East Anglia, but for my own part I retraced my steps to its junction with the curiously named Unthank Road, where I sank into a pub; three churches in two hours is a lot, and there was still the cathedral ahead.

Revived physically and morally by a glass of sherry which had cost only 2s. 3d., I headed back to St. Giles, re-entering the city through St. Giles' Gate—of which no trace remains, nor of the medieval walls at that point—and noticing, this time, at the side of the church Cow Hill, which leads to the junction with Willow Lane and the house in which George Borrow, a Norfolk man, lived in his youth; he was for two years at Norwich Grammar School, and was afterwards articled to a firm of Norwich solicitors.

Back at the Guildhall I inquired the way to the cathedral, and the citizen I addressed instructed me to go along 'London Lane', which he pointed out to me, with a tailoring establishment on the corner. It proved to be a narrow winding street of shops and offices, but it was called street, not lane. I thought the shops, as I went along, rather good, and afterwards learned that London Street is known as the local Bond Street. I also thought, as I continued on, that I had never seen so many insurance and building society offices in my life, and inescapably dominating the commercial scene, the Norwich Union Assurance Company, which aroused memories of the 'Mancroft case' of a few years ago, when the Arab Boycott Office banned the Norwich Union—not because the chairman, Lord Mancroft, was a Jew, but because the company had dealings with 'Israel'. But Norwich is proud of its financial institutions, and the Norwich Union finds a place in the Official Guide as the concern 'which has helped above all to make the name of Norwich famous'. It was founded in 1797 by a wine merchant and banker called Thomas Bignold, and was expanded into a national concern by his son, Samuel. Their great new building, south of the City Centre, is prized as the city's first high building. . . .

The cathedral is reached by way of Tombland, which has nothing to do with tombs, but is a pleasant square with trees and old houses, and a church, and at either end a gateway to the Cathedral Close, the Ethelbert Gate and the Erpingham Gate. Tombland was the site of the Saxon market, and was a *toom*, an open piece of land. The Ethelbert Gate, by which I entered, is thirteenth century, and the older of the two gates, but unlike the other does not lead directly to the cathedral, but through the gardens of the close, pleasant with lawns and trees and flower-beds, and past various monastic buildings. The Ethelbert Gate was built as an act of penance by the citizens of Norwich following 'town and gown riots' between the populace, allied with the soldiery, and the servants of the cathedral priory. The mob set fire to the gates and then to the priory, and the flames spread to a part of the cathedral itself.

When all this disorderly conduct was over there were hangings for murder and sacrilege, Henry III deprived the citizens of their liberties, and the Pope laid Norwich under an interdict; a huge fine had to be paid to the Vatican, and the Ethelbert Gate built as a penance. The gate as it exists today is much as it was in the thirteenth century, but the flint gable is a nineteenth-century restoration. It is usual to approach the cathedral by the other gate, built by 'good old Sir Thomas Erpingham', who commanded the archers at Agincourt; it was built in 1420, and in a niche set into the gable there is a statue of Sir Thomas. Through the gate you come immediately to the west front of the cathedral; it was, and is, the accepted public approach; the Ethelbert Gate led to the monastery. None of this I knew at the time; I went in at Ethelbert because it was the gate to which I came through Tombland.

The Cathedral Church of the Holy and Undivided Trinity was founded by Herbert de Losinga, who thereby became first bishop of Norwich, at the end of the eleventh century. It has the nobility of all Norman cathedrals, but was not for me as exciting as York or Winchester—perhaps because of its bareness; it suffered very much at the hands of the Puritans during the Civil War. Perhaps its greatest treasure is the Erpingham Window, in the presbytery in the north aisle, which is an assemblage of medieval Norwich glass from various sources and donors; the work was carried out by a Norwich firm in 1963.

What I did find exciting were the cloisters, which I didn't

know at the time are considered the largest and most beautiful in the country, but which seemed to me most wonderful.

Remarkable, too, and memorable, are the great flying buttresses which you see when you leave the cathedral by the south door. You are then in the curiously named Life's Green, and here is the modest grave of Nurse Cavell, tucked away in a corner, with a simple cross and growing flowers—pansies, when I was there. There is a bust on a pedestal of this heroine of the First World War at the junction of Wensum Street and Palace Street, facing the Bishop's Palace.

A little farther down is the Erpingham Gate, and across from it a half-timbered house and an archway; through the arch is Tombland Alley, with sixteenth-century houses. The bulging and leaning house on the right as you go in under the arch is the house of Augustine Steward, who governed Norwich in 1549 when the mayor had been carried off by Robert Kett and his fellow rebels who were encamped twenty thousand strong on Mousehold Heath to the north-east of the city, in their struggle against the injustice of the enclosure of common lands. The house of Augustine Steward became the H.Q. of the armies sent to crush the rebellion. Kett held out for a month, then was captured and hanged from the battlements of Norwich Castle. Then on the fourth centenary of the rebellion, in 1949, the city reversed the judgment, and from being a traitor Kett was acknowledged a fighter for justice, and given a plaque at the castle gate: *In 1549 A.D. Robert Kett yeoman farmer of Wymondham was executed by hanging in this castle after the defeat of the Norfolk Rebellion of which he was the leader. In 1949 A.D., four hundred years later, this memorial was placed here by the citizens of Norwich in reparation and honour to a notable and courageous leader in the long struggle of the common people of England to escape from a servile life into the freedom of just conditions.*

Tombland Alley leads round the churchyard of St. George's Tombland Church to Prince's Street, where there are some attractive Tudor houses at one side of the road and at the other the square glass modern block of a shoe factory. Here, too, is the entrance to a museum which was once the church of St. Peter Hungate; when this beautiful church became redundant it was taken over by the municipality and is now full of treasures and curiosities from churches all over Norfolk, and is open, free, to the public.

Behind the church museum is Elm Hill, all fifteenth-century houses and antique shops. If you follow it along its cobbled way it brings you to the Maid's Head Hotel and the Edith Cavell statue. I had thought this black and white inn a fake, and it seems that the façade is, replacing a Georgian one, which is a very great pity, but before it became the Maid's Head Hotel and one of the places in which the first Queen Elizabeth is supposed to have slept, it had an honest pedigree as the Myrtle Fish Tavern going back to the reign of Edward III, when ships were built for the Royal Navy beside the River Wensum, crossed by a bridge farther up the road.

I retraced my steps to Tombland and back to the castle where I headed out south along the endlessness of Ber Street with the idea of getting out to Bracondale and the best section of the remaining city walls. If you keep on long enough you come to Carrow Hill and the remains of a tower by Carrow Bridge across the river, which sweeps round the city in a great loop. But though I came to some railinged-off remains of city walls, near a pub called Ber Streate Gate, I gave up before reaching Bracondale; it was beginning to rain, and I had been trekking for hours all over the city and there comes a point at which both energy and interest give out, and I had reached it. I had had enough; Ber Street was too drab and straight and went on too long, and it was a long walk back to the City Centre, to circle the castle once again and dip down to the Prince of Wales Road, full of people and shops and red buses, and at the end of it Thorpe Station and the London train.

I should have seen King Street, of course, said to be the oldest street in Norwich; it is another long straight street marching south, parallel with the river; the Old Barge Inn is there, fourteenth century, timbered, and reputedly a very fine specimen of the period; and there are other fine medieval houses, and the even older Old Music House, the oldest dwelling-house in Norwich, and one of the oldest in the country; it was built in the twelfth century by a wealthy Jew known as Moses the Jew. But what is important in Norwich is the castle area, with the market place, and Tombland and the cathedral. There are thirty-three mediaeval churches in Norwich; it is too much. Like the preponderance of insurance offices.

The Official Guide declares proudly that Norwich is a 'provincial capital in a sense that can scarcely be applied to any other English city. From forty miles round people come to it for their marketing, business and recreation.' All those mediaeval houses and churches, and the great Norman cathedral, and the Norman castle and market place; undoubtedly it all adds up to a great and interesting provincial capital. Yet in retrospect what I liked best were the little blossoming wistaria trees ringed round the church of St. Giles-on-the-Hill, the wistaria church. . . .

13

Winchester, the Ancient Capital

APART from the fact that it is, perhaps, the most beautiful of all our old cathedral cities, Winchester has a place in this book as the ancient and original capital. As late as the thirteenth century it was still only second in importance to London. Its earliest history is lost in antiquity and legend; it is associated with King Arthur and his Knights; it was the capital of the kings of Wessex, when Wessex was the leading kingdom in the land. It is the city of St. Swithun who, as bishop, ordered the building of the great wall round the cathedral, as protection against the Danish invaders in the year 860, two years before his death. Canute was buried there, and his wife, Emma, bequeathed her house, the Manor of Godbegot, to the cathedral. William the Conqueror, although he had himself crowned at Westminster, had a royal palace built at Winchester and set up administrative offices there. All this and much more, not forgetting the Romans, when it was Venta Belgarum, an important Romano-British market town.

When you arrive in the city as a stranger, as I did without even a map, all is as easy as arriving in the city of York, for all is immediately there; you cannot go wrong. No 'bus to the City Centre is involved; you take the road ahead of you when you come out of the City Railway Station, and, following it round into Jewry Street, come in a few minutes to the High Street;

you then have the choice of turning right and going uphill to the city gate which you see at the top, and which is Westgate, or going left down to the City Cross, with the cathedral behind. I went up to Westgate, because I realised that all that area down there, with the cathedral and the college, was going to take a little time—much more than whatever there was up there by Westgate.

The west gate is one of the two remaining gates of the city walls; the other is Kingsgate, which is the south gate. There were originally five of these massive medieval gates; the two that remain are in a good state of preservation. On the west gate, at the side facing away from the High Street, there is a groove for a portcullis, and two grotesque heads from whose open mouths had come the chains for the drawbridge. On the High Street side, to the left of the central arch, is an entrance, and a flight of stone stairs leads up to what is now a museum. There is a collection of old weights and measures, armour, a set of gibbeting irons—used as late as 1834, when gibbeting was abolished—some fifteenth-century stained glass in the windows, and scratched on the grey stone walls the names of people imprisoned there in the sixteenth, seventeenth and eighteenth centuries. Another flight of stone stairs leads up to the roof, which is the top of the west wall, from which there is a fine view out over the city to the Hampshire downs behind. From here is to be seen the cathedral, with its low square tower, at the heart of the city, and beyond it the tall pinnacled tower of the chapel of Winchester College, and, a green backcloth to grey towers and clustered red roofs, the long ridge of hills, bare except for a clump of trees, reminiscent of Chanctonbury Ring, which marks the top of St. Catherine's Hill and the site of a mediaeval chapel, founded in honour of St. Catherine. The trees are beeches, planted in 1762. I had no time on that first visit to go up the hill, but did so later in the year. Half way up traces of the earthwork of the settlement which existed there about 300 B.C. are to be made out in the

L

shape of a ridge encircling the hill and known as the 'parapets'. There is also clearly discernible—though overgrown—a turf labyrinth, the 'miz-maze', possibly mediaeval.

A short distance from Westgate, up a narrow turning, there is an imposing red-roofed building with mullioned windows which at first glance suggests a church; it stands back across a courtyard and commands the same view as from the roof of Westgate. It is the Castle Hall, all that remains of a castle built at the time of William the Conqueror; it fell to Cromwell after a six days' siege in 1645 and was demolished by order of Parliament within the next few years; the Hall was put to various uses, including that of law court. It was here that the notorious Judge Jeffreys held the 'Bloody Assizes' in 1685. It is now again in use as a court of law, though only temporarily, pending the construction of four new courts, which means that by the time this appears in print the interior is no longer disfigured with sheets of boarding and hoarding dividing it into offices and screening off the law courts. It was not open to the public the day I was there, because the court was sitting, but an obliging policeman offered 'as a favour' to show me a window through which I would be able to see 'King Arthur's Table'. The Hall was finished in 1235 and is considered the finest thirteenth-century aisled hall in the country, in the Early English style. Certainly what I could see of it, as I followed the policeman in, was tremendously impressive, with its immensly high pillars and lofty ceiling. Through a window in one of the temporary offices 'King Arthur's Round Table,' high up on a wall under some small stained-glass windows, looked like a huge darts board. It is eighteen feet in diameter and marked off with spaces for King Arthur and his twenty-four knights, whose names are inscribed around the edges. At the centre is a Tudor rose, painted for the visit of the Emperor Charles V in 1522. As a relic of King Arthur it is undoubtedly phoney, and the fifteenth-century chronicler John Hardyng referred to it simply as 'The rounde Table of Wynchester', but the words 'and there it hangeth yet' suggests that it was already an antiquity at that time. If it has nothing to do with the historical Arthur, Winchester is anyhow indissolubly linked with the Arthurian legend, and since that is all part of Wessex, what is wrong with that?

Across the road from Westgate is Elizabeth II Court, the new Hampshire County Council offices, designed in 1936 and completed in 1959, and opened in that year by the Queen. The main building is three-storeyed of good, darkish red brick, with a long red-tiled roof, from which rises a four-sided clock-tower, surmounted by a weather-vane. The whole forms a very handsome group of buildings, simple but dignified, and with a certain 'Scandinavian' elegance. Winchester, which was untouched by the Industrial Revolution, has been so far blessedly spared the ʼrutal ugliness of high square blocks of offices and flats which all over the world have become symbols of the crass materialism of our age, and these mid-twentieth-century municipal buildings, with their clear, graceful lines, strike no discordant note in that thirteenth-century castle area. There is a certain amount of nondescript building around, but it is insignificant; the scene is dominated by the handsome mediaeval stone gateway, and the distinguished modern brick municipal buildings.

In the middle of the cross-roads there stands a monument commemorating the Great Plague in the city in 1666. It is in the form of a small obelisk, and engraved on the side facing the west gate are the words: *This Monument is Erected by the Society of Natives on the very Spot of Ground to which the Markets were removed and whose Basis is the very stone on which Exchanges were made whilst the City lay under the Scourge of the Destroying Pestilence in the Year Sixteen Hundred and Sixty Six.*

It was rebuilt in 1821, and repaired in 1869.

A roadsweeper, watching me with close interest whilst I copied the inscription, remarked as I closed my notebook, 'The place is full of history—everywhere you go!'

Going down from there, down Upper High Street to the

High Street proper, you come to the Manor of Godbegot, now a hotel and restaurant. Beside it is Royal Oak Passage, all that is left of Alwarene Street, the eastern boundary of the Jewish ghetto, until the Jews were expelled from England in 1290. The Manor extends along this passageway, its first storey projecting on massive beams over the small ground-floor windows—now the windows of the hotel kitchen; only this side of the house is ancient, the rest having been so heavily restored at different periods that nothing of the original structure remains. An inscription on the wall on the passage side says that in 1012 it was the property of 'Alfric the Goodsgetter'; it was Ethelred, Emma's first husband, who made her a present of the Manor, and this Alfric is only a shadowy former owner, not mentioned in the archives until 1052, the year of Emma's death.

The Royal Oak pub is at the other side of the passageway, and contains what it claims is the oldest bar in England. It is a cellar-like room down some ancient stone steps from the ground floor of the pub, and the landlord gives the date as 1050. There are the remains of a flint stone wall at one side and part of an archway can be traced. The massive beams, says the landlord, are Elizabethan. He points with pride to a pair of handsome eighteenth-century spirit jars—'from the days when a tot of gin cost a penny!' One of the two ladies who has descended the stone steps with me murmurs something about gin palaces and mother's ruin; her companion inquires cryptically whether the dense cobwebs in the lattice window behind the jars are also the oldest in England ... The inn-keeper takes it all in good part. They're modern, he acknowledges, cheerfully. I ask him whether the bar is still used, and he says, why, certainly, at nights it's full. It's cold down there, and dark, and we are glad to go back up the worn steps to the bright and cheerful ordinariness of the lounge bar, into which the sunshine filters from the passageway.

Across the road there is the old Guildhall, come down in the world and now a bank. It stands on the corner of a side turning. St. Thomas Street, where a plaque says that *this building became the Hall of Court on or about 1361, replacing a building further west in the High Street. In late years it was known as the Guildhall and was rebuilt in 1711. The town clock and the Queen Anne statue* (this is high up on the High Street façade of the building) *date from 1713. Here hangs the city's curfew bell, which is still rung at 8 p.m. each weekday.*

The statue and the town clock were gifts from two Members of Parliament for the city in the year of the Peace of Utrecht, which terminated the war with France. Inscribed under the statue are the words: *Anno Pacifico Anna Regina, 1713*. Narrow St. Thomas Street, with its pleasant eighteenth-century houses, I found reminiscent of the Palants of Chichester—Winchester is altogether reminiscent of Chichester, but because of its setting is more beautiful. The site on which the old Guildhall stood, and which is now Lloyd's Bank, was first recorded in 1295 as the site of a large group of cottages and an inn. There is still an inn, the Dolphin pub, at the opposite corner of St. Thomas Street, with a timbered and projecting first storey on the High Street side, but the rest of the building is of doubtful antiquity. There is a general confusion of styles and periods, but the effect remains of an interesting and attractive high street, nevertheless.

A short distance down there is the City Cross, graceful in its ornate Gothic fashion, with steps up to it and surmounted by a cross. The Official Guide declares firmly that it was erected in the fifteenth century and restored in 1865, but Barbara Carpenter Turner, in her Pitkin Pictorial book on Winchester,[1] says that 'no one knows how or when the High Cross was first set up in the city. Much of the original structure has gone, but a date of about 1450 has been suggested'. She adds that 'the Cross may have been a gift from a bishop or a king, or may be the citizens' commemoration of their city's recovery from the Black Death'. At Westgate I had inquired of a citizen where

1. 1967.

was the other remaining gate, and he had told me to 'go down to the Butter Cross', and directed me from there. According to the Official Guide it is so-called 'because of its former market trading associations'. The Guide says also that 'a neighbouring landowner bought the Cross in 1770 for his wife's landscape garden and it was saved for the city only by a timely rally of the citizens who drove off the workmen as they were about to carry it away'.

The Cross has houses of different periods behind and at the side of it, their ground floors converted to shops, and an arched passageway which leads into the Square, where again there are houses of various periods, sixteenth, seventeenth and eighteenth century. On the righthand side of the passageway there is a plaque which says that here stood William the Conqueror's palace, some Norman stones from which were re-used in the building of the chimney-breast to the left of the plaque. At the other side of the passageway is the little fifteenth-century church of St. Lawrence, 'the mother church, built upon the site of the Palace of William the Conqueror', according to the plaque; but according to the leaflet available in the church it was built on the site of the chapel of the palace. In 1140, when the city was destroyed by fire, the Bishop of Winchester had the stones of the royal chapel and palace removed to strengthen his castle south-east of the cathedral. Ten years later, when a parish of St. Lawrence was established, the Chapel Royal was rebuilt as the parish church. The Bishop then ordered that the church should have all the land formerly occupied by the Conqueror's palace. Today the church owns only the land on which it stands. In 1449 the church was completely rebuilt, and, according to the leaflet, 'succeeding centuries saw much decay and ruin to the fabric of the church until a major restoration was put in hand in 1849 and further work was carried out in the 1950's'.

The church has a raftered ceiling, and is plain and bare, but the east window is Perpendicular, with stained glass and, though much restored, is beautiful. In general the interest of the church is historical rather than architectural. The rectory of the church is round the corner and is now a pub called the Eclipse Inn, an attractive timbered building, shamelessly announcing along its frontage that it was once the rectory . . . but this so olde worlde building is in fact a modern restoration. The inn was called the Eclipse in opposition to its rival, the Sun. . . .

It is very pleasant here, in the cathedral precincts, with the grey beauty of the cathedral in its setting of lawns and trees, and the narrow lanes of streets—Little Minster Street, and Great Minster Street—with old houses of different periods, and little shops with casement or bow windows—the more interesting kind of shops, art shops, antique shops, book shops, a shop selling children's clothes. Great Minster Street, facing on to the Cathedral Close, is very attractive, and, says Barbara Carpenter Turner, 'hardly altered since the early nineteenth century'. At the other end, at the junction with Little Minster Street, there are beautiful old flint walls, made more beautiful still in the month of May with clematis crowding over, cascades of delicate starry flowers and curling tendrils, and occasional outcrops of wistaria, a loveliness of mauve blossom, exquisitely frail, on rough grey stone. Behind these flint walls enclosing gardens rise the upper storeys and red roofs of old and gracious houses.

There was everywhere, that May afternoon of sun and cloud, an almost overpowering scent of the small white clematis that trailed its bridal beauty over garden walls and the walls of old houses. I turned almost reluctantly in at the gates of the cathedral grounds; there were red and white hawthorn trees, thick with blossom, and giving out their own sweet scent, and there were lawns thick with daisies, and a copper beech glowing in the sunshine, and children playing on the grass . . . and the great cathedral waited. Well, it had waited for the half a century of my adult life, and it could wait a little longer now; I was afraid of it; once I had gone in I would be committed in the course of the next few days or weeks to getting something of its greatness down on to paper, and the more beautiful anything is, whether it is scenery or a cathedral or a piece of music, the more difficult it is to pin it down in words. Therefore I postponed the cathedral and went haring off behind it in search of that gate about which I had inquired earlier, Kingsgate, to the south, the King's Gate, where a long stretch of the city wall still stands.

It is easily enough found on leaving the Cathedral Close, for it is just outside, with the tiny mediaeval Church of St. Swithun above it—St. Swithun-upon-Kingsgate. A plaque on the gate says that it is one of the five large city gates, and is mentioned in 1148, but that 'the present structure is possibly of the fourteenth century'. A short flight of stairs lead up into the church, and you are then on top of the city wall.

I liked this tiny church very much. It has a raftered ceiling, ribbed like an inverted boat, and is simple and plain; in such a church it is possible to feel at home. I sat down in a pew and made some notes, from the information provided on a tablet. The church is one of only four such churches remaining today, and was built in 1263, on the original ancient gateway of the twelfth century. In 1337 the woodwork was overhauled by two carpenters and two sawyers, who worked for four weeks at a total cost of fifteen shillings. In 1484 the windows were mended at a cost of four shillings and sixpence. In 1660 the church was restored, and again in 1959 'major restoration was undertaken at a very high cost' . . . and the rector appeals for help.

The east window contains ancient glass from the church of St. Peter, at Chesil-in-the-Soke, now disused. The Soke, it should be said, was the jurisdiction set up by the bishopric when much of the city was royal demesne; property which came under the jurisdiction of the Soke acknowledged only the bishop as overlord.

Something, perhaps, should be said, too, about St. Swithun,

of whom it is proverbially said that it if rains on his day it will rain for forty days after. Apart from being the bishop responsible for the wall being built round the cathedral in the ninth century he was reputedly a good and holy and humble man who had no wish to be given a noble tomb in the cathedral in due course, and who in accordance with his wish was originally buried outside, in 862; when the grave was opened for his remains to be re-interred in the cathedral, on July 15, 971, the heavens wept their protest for forty days thereafter.

A memorial tablet in St. Swithun-upon-Kingsgate I liked so much that I copied it out: it was removed from the church of St. Maurice, now demolished, and placed there, with other memorials, during restoration work in 1955–61: *To the memory of William Widmore. He was (which is most rare) a friend without guile, an Apothecary without ostentation, his extensive Charity in his Profession entitled him to be called the Physician of the poor. Let other inscriptions boast Honnours, Pedigrees and Riches. Here lies an honest Englishman, who died the 19th day of June 1756, aged 63.*

When you go through Kingsgate you find that a modern house has been built up to the gate, and in this area of beautiful old houses and the high flint walls of the Cathedral Close it is momentarily disconcerting, but it is of a good modern design, and where the sixteenth, seventeenth and eighteenth centuries jumble together there can perhaps be no objection to the twentieth cropping up, and this 'contemporary' house which adjoins the mediaeval gate is anyhow to be preferred to the nondescript building adjoining it. With this philosophical reflection I turned left into College Street, which is altogether delightful, with tulip trees against the grey stone walls of old houses, and a happy conglomeration of old red brick, red tiles, grey flint, and always the cascades of the starry clematis, with its sweet pursuing scent.

At the other side of the road, just before you get to the college, a plaque on the wall of a small square house announces that Jane Austen lived her last days there, dying there on July 18, 1817. She had come to Winchester for medical treatment and had worked there on her last novel, *Persuasion*, which was published posthumously.

The famous public school, founded by Bishop William of Wykeham in 1382, part of the city's revival after the devastation of the Black Death, in which half the population died, has its main entrance here in College Street, with an ancient statue of the Virgin, patron saint of the college, above the archway. In the quadrangle beyond, a few boys wearing gowns drifted about and others sat on a bench under a sunny wall. I found myself wondering if they realised the wonderful surroundings in which they were being educated, all red brick and grey stone— it was rather like Hampton Court, I thought, and the chapel with its splendid tower noble enough for a cathedral. The cloisters are very beautiful; the War Cloister is modern, designed by Sir Herbert Baker, the architect of New Delhi; it was built to commemorate the 500 Wykehamists killed in the First World War, and the names of those who died in the Second World War were added. The chapel now has a modern armoured glass entrance door, framed in metal to form a cross: it was installed as recently as January, 1967. The windows are Perpendicular, with richly coloured glass; the east window is a nineteenth-century copy of the original.

Continuing on down College Street you come, on the opposite side of the road, to a fine house lying back in some gardens, and behind the house a chapel, and behind that again some ruins: the house is Wolvesey House, designed by Wren as a palace for Bishop Morley; the ruins are of Wolvesey Castle, built by Henry de Blois, half-brother of King Stephen, Bishop of Winchester in 1138. Henry de Blois had a dream of making Winchester into an archbishopric, rivalling Canterbury. The castle was dismantled after the Civil War, and the palace was begun by Wren in 1684. The remaining wing of the palace is the home of the bishops of Winchester. Playing fields adjoin the palace grounds, and behind rises a wooded hill. The castle ruins were closed to visitors when I was there, 'whilst work is in progress'.

Unable to view the ruins I turned back, retracing my steps to the cathedral. Back, then, through Kingsgate, and the gate of the Close, very near it, past the beautiful gabled and half-timbered Cheyney Court, where the courts of the Soke were held, presided over by the bishop's steward, and so into the cathedral through the entrance in the south transept—the Cathedral Church of the Holy Trinity, St. Peter, St. Paul and St. Swithun. It is entering in the middle, of course, and brings you almost immediately to the staggering chief glory of the cathedral, which is the elaborately carved and magnificent high altar screen, but if you come in at the west front, with the great nave stretching ahead of you, with the east window rising clearly above the tremendous reredos, that is staggering, too. This is not the cathedral round which the good bishop Swithun, two years before his death, had the great wall built, but the Norman cathedral of Bishop Walkelyn, who succeeded the last Anglo-Saxon bishop, Stigand, in 1070, and in 1079 began the construction of the new cathedral, the largest church in western Europe, saving only the old St. Paul's Cathedral. In the north and south transepts the Norman building is virtually unchanged; the south transept has had the addition of two late mediaeval chapels, but the north transept is, after eight centuries, as Bishop Walkelyn built it.

The cathedral suffered very badly at the hands of Cromwell's men during the Civil War, and it was even proposed by Parliament at one point to demolish it completely; it was saved by a petition of the townspeople. The reredos was denuded of figures and remained so until the nineteenth century, when it was restored. Much of the glass is modern, though some fragments of fourteenth-century glass were preserved in the west window. The effigy of William of Wykeham on his tomb in the south aisle of the nave escaped destruction, due, it is said, to the fact that the captain of the Cromwellian troops who ravaged the cathedral was himself a Wykehamist . . . The alabaster effigy of Bishop Edington, who began the reconstruction of the south nave aisle from the Norman to the Gothic style, was damaged, the feet being smashed, but is still very fine.

I find it, really, impossible adequately to describe this cathedral. Not only is it of staggering beauty in its loftiness and grace, but it contains too much, too many chapels and chantries and tombs and shrines; I made notes of a few things that specially interested me as I went round; I noted the chapel of William of Wykeham, half way along the south aisle; the mortuary chests containing the bones of King Canute and Emma, and some of the early kings of Wessex and bishops of Winchester; the reredos of the Lady Chapel, which is a memorial to Charlotte Yonge, 1823–1901, and the early sixteenth-century wall paintings depicting the legends of the Virgin. I noted the marble tablet in the floor marking the spot where Jane Austen is buried and learned from it that she was only forty-one when she died. Another literary association is Izaak Walton, who was buried in Prior Silkstede's Chapel in the south transept on December 19, 1683. A marble slab marks his grave, and the handsome stained-glass window is a memorial given by fishermen in many lands in 1914. He is depicted in the right- and left-hand corners at the bottom. A woman with a French accent asked me if I could tell her where was the tomb of William Rufus, and as I had just been looking at it I was able to take her to it, in the middle of the choir—though I was not able to tell her then what I only discovered later, which is that it is only 'known as' the tomb of Rufus, and has also been believed to be the tomb of Bishop Henry de Blois.

These are only a few things; there is much, much more; these notes must serve only as indications. One takes in the things that interest one personally, and the rest the saturated mind will not hold. Absurdly, and if you like significantly, I have remembered a tombstone outside, in memory of a young soldier of the Hampshire militia, Thomas Thetcher, who died in the month of May, in the eighteenth century, 'of a violent fever contracted by drinking Small Beer when hot'. The stone was placed there by his comrades at their expense as a testimony of their 'regard and concern'. I liked very much the verse inscribed on this memorial:

> *Here sleeps in peace a Hampshire Grenadier*
> *Who caught his death by drinking cold small beer.*
> *Soldiers be wise from his untimely fall*
> *And when yere hot drink Strong or none at all.*

The poor young man—he was only twenty-six—died in 1764, but the memorial being decayed by 1787 was 'restored by the Officers of the Garrison', and another two lines of verse were added:

> *An honest Soldier never is forgot*
> *Whether he die by Musket or by Pot.*

This seemed to me a very fine tribute, and a right attitude of mind, but it was not the end of the story of the memorial to poor Tom Thetcher, for a final inscription declares: *This stone was placed by the North Hants Militia when disembodied at Winchester on 26th April 1802, in consequence of the original Stone being destroyed.*

I suppose I shall remember that long after I have forgotten the details of Norman splendours and medieval masterpieces. A teetotaller would point the moral; a fellow-drinker can only stand by the grave and in spirit raise a tankard and murmur, Alas, poor Tom!

For anyone moved to go and symbolically shed a tear or lay a flower, the tombstone is to be found by a group of yew trees at the righthand side of the avenue of limes leading to the west front of the cathedral.

At the other end of this avenue of ancient limes—they are reputedly three hundred years old—there is the City Museum, where you can trace the history of Winchester from King Alfred to Queen Victoria, and where there are Jane Austen relics, and Wren's plan for a palace for Charles II; but I cannot report at first-hand on all this because I did not go in, having an assignation with some almshouses away out across the water-meadows at the other side of the city.

I knew these almshouses of St. Cross were somewhere out beyond the water-meadows; what I had not known was where these water-meadows were. I had inquired of one of the Friends of the Cathedral, a pleasant woman seated at a table near the bookstall, and she had been friendly and helpful. Did I know Wolvesey? I said I had not long come from there. Then I would know College Walk, the turning opposite; all I had to do was to follow it until I came to the stream—the old college mill stream—and follow it out across the meadows until I came to a road, cross the road and continue to follow the stream. I would have the River Itchen away over to my left. It was, she had concluded, warmly, a delightful walk.

I am sure it is—provided the heavens don't open as they did that afternoon before I had crossed from the college, at the end of the Walk, into the meadows. I ran for shelter into a porch, where a youngish woman with a baby in a pram, and two dogs on a lead, was sheltering. The dogs barked, the baby crowed, the mother smiled, ruefully. We agreed that it wasn't the sort of rain you could go through. I told her I very much wanted to see St. Cross before getting my train back to town; I'd been told it wasn't much more than about fifteen minutes' walk from here. It was rather more than that, she said, more like half an hour. I replied that I would go, all the same, as I understood the almshouses were very fine. She agreed that they were, adding that they still gave the traditional 'wayfarer's dole' of ale and bread, though, of course, it was only a token taste of beer, just a tiny glass. I was amused by the idea, but doubted if I would want beer in the afternoon—and a wet one at that.

I peered through the deep modern window that flanked the porch and inquired what was within, and learned that it was the new assembly hall, and, as my co-shelterer observed, it was a pity I could not pass the time until the rain was over by going in and having a look round, but the door was locked. She drew my attention, however, to some sections of panelling and a carved screen which had originally been in the college chapel; it seemed it was seventeenth-century wood-carving and had been removed from the chapel in the late nineteenth century and, most improperly, sold; fortunately it was eventually recovered, and it was decided to install it in the New Hall instead of replacing it in the chapel. She mentioned, as though to account for knowing all this, that her husband was chaplain. I didn't, then, reveal my own identity—it would have involved explanations and I was not in the mood—but later, seeking some information, I wrote to 'the chaplain', asking if he would be so good as to pass the letter to his wife, with whom, I said, I had sheltered from the rain. She replied very cordially and helpfully, and I learned that there are three chaplains, and have been since the fourteenth century, and that there are now, also, three chapels, one of which was a disused parish church, recently acquired. The main chapel was built for the original seventy scholars of the foundation, and is not big enough for the present roll of 530. The second chapel is known as Chantry; it is officially Fromond's Chantry, and was built between 1420 and 1445 by the executors of John Fromond, Steward of the College, for masses to be sung in it for the repose of his soul, and the souls of his wife and friends.

All this I learned later; that wet afternoon in the porch of the New Hall I knew only that my co-shelterer was 'the chaplain's wife', and she knew only that I was a visitor from London, there for the day, and doggedly determined to walk to St. Cross in spite of the deluge.

When the rain appeared to let up a little I said that I thought I had better start swimming out across those water-meadows, and I said goodbye and left the friendly shelter of the porch, crossed the road, passed in through a small iron gate and proceeded to follow the stream, as instructed. Across the meadows threaded by the little River Itchen the green hill of St. Catherine's rises in the near distance; this is one of Winchester's most beautiful and famous views, and it was just a pity that that afternoon the rain came on heavily again, blurring it.

With the rain in my face I plunged on along the narrow path beside the stream, and it seemed a long time before I came to the road; there were occasional houses lying back across the fields at the other side of the stream, but nothing which looked like almshouses. I came to the road at last and crossed it, and remembered that the lady in the cathedral had said that when I had done so I should follow the stream again. But now there were apparently two streams—the one I had been following and parallel with it a narrower one. But where was the path? It was a few moments before I realised that the narrower one was the path. Then, telling myself that the beauty of being wet through is that you cannot become any wetter, I splashed down into it.

This section of the water-meadows—and they seemed aptly named—also seemed to go on for a long time, and when I came to a small bridge leading to a road and some houses I decided I had had enough of the meadows and crossed the bridge; the road led, after a few yards, to a narrower one called Back Street. At the end of this street there loomed up grey buildings which could be almshouses or their precincts. I inquired of a woman letting herself into a house if St. Cross was down that way and she replied, shaking the water from her umbrella, that she thought so.

It was a curious reply, even if she was a stranger there herself, because not only the almshouses but the whole area there is St. Cross, once the village of Sparkford, but becoming known

as St. Cross when St. Cross Hospital was founded in 1137 by
Bishop Henry de Blois for 'thirteen poor impotent men so
reduced in strength as rarely or never to be able to raise themselves without the assistance of another'. In 1445 the Cardinal
Bishop, Henry de Beaufort, added a second foundation, the
Almhouse of Noble Poverty. De Blois' pensioners wear a
black gown and silver cross of Jerusalem; Beaufort's a claret-
coloured gown and a badge surmounted by a cardinal's hat;
these uniforms are worn to this day.

You come first to a gatehouse, in which there is the porter's
lodge; beyond is a courtyard, and across it rises the fifteenth-
century tower of Cardinal Beaufort, with an entrance arch
under it into the beautiful grassy quadrangle round two sides of
which the almshouses are built, of grey stone, with tall chimneys; on the left as you enter is a cloister-like covered way,
leading down to the church, which forms the fourth side of the
quadrangle, facing Beaufort's tower. The church is known as
the Chapel of St. Cross; it is considered to be 'unequalled as an
example of transitional Norman work', though parts of the
church are later, Early English or Decorated. The interior is
noble and beautiful, but I was too wet and cold to take in anything in detail. The whole place is extremely beautiful, and
claims to be the finest medieval almshouse in the country; certainly there could hardly be any collection of buildings more
harmonious in their long low design, with the tall chimneys and
mullioned windows, or anything more suggestive of a cloistered serenity. Bishop de Blois housed thirteen needy aged men,
and provided, additionally, a hundred dinners daily. Today
there are twenty-seven pensioners resident in the two foundations, and many out-pensioners.

The traditional 'dole' is to be had on application at the
porter's lodge, but I did not ask for it, or even to be shown over
the almshouses—which is permitted—because, wet through
and with squelching shoes, I had no heart for prolonging the
visit, and the thought of even a small glass of cold clammy beer

M

was repellent. I could have used a rum-grog, but would have settled for a hot cup of tea. A face looked out from a window but it was a face that wasn't going to offer either, and I turned damply away.

I decided not to paddle back across the so watery water-meadows, but to follow the parallel road. The narrow roads of St. Cross, flanked by small and attractive old houses, soon give way to the long Kingsgate Road, which, followed to the end, comes out, as might be expected, at Kingsgate.

Before it was clear to me that this long road was the one I wanted I inquired of a van driver loading goods into a house if I was going right for the town centre.

'That's it,' he reassured me. 'Keep going till you come to an archway. At the other side you'll see a big church—well, it's a cathedral really—'

'Ah, yes,' I interrupted him. 'I know where I am when I get there . . .'

It had ceased raining by the time I got back to the big church. The avenue of lime trees at the far side of the Close dripped mightily, but the air was full of sweet scents of rain-drenched blossoms and a thanksgiving chorus of birds.

If, instead of turning off the High Street in the middle to enter the Cathedral Close, you continue on down you find it widening into the Broadway, in the middle of which is a bronze statue of King Alfred, standing with his shield on a stone plinth. It was put up in 1901 to commemorate the thousandth anniversary of Alfred's death. Across from it is the Victorian Gothic building of the Guildhall, all spires and towers, and adjoining it is beautiful Abbey House, the residence of the Mayor. It is of brick, with a tower at each end, and a stream flowing past. A small public gardens adjoins it, and house and gardens are on part of the site of a Benedictine foundation of St. Mary's Abbey, sometimes referred to as Nunnaminster, a nunnery founded by Alswitha, the wife of Alfred.

Across the road a little farther on the High Street ends with a small humped stone bridge over the river, built in 1813 and replacing the first city bridge, built by St. Swithun, 852–63. At the other side of it is the gabled red brick house which was the City Mill, and which is now a youth hostel. At the corner of the road, over the bridge, stands the beautiful fifteenth-century house which was Old Chesil Rectory, now a café. It was the rectory of St. Peter Chesil Church—now closed—which stands at the other side of the road, Chesil Street, the street of the chesil or strand of the River Itchen. The house, which is gabled and half-timbered, used to be two cottages; it was restored in 1893.

At the other side of the bridge there is the riverside walk known as the Weirs, a very pleasant walk through gardens and following not only the river but the medieval city wall, part of which enclosed the bishop's castle of Wolvesey. Following the wall round you come out facing College Walk, and in College Street, leading on to Kingsgate, the wall merges into beautiful old stone houses; Jane Austen's house faces the last of the wall. The beautiful old house of the Pilgrim's School is passed just after Wolvesey, enclosed behind high flint stone walls, and facing the main entrance to the college. Back at Kingsgate you come to the high walls of the Cathedral Close, and if you have begun at Westgate have done the circuit of the ancient capital, and England's loveliest city.

14

Liverpool, the Swinging City

WITH Liverpool as with Dover I was returning for a closer look at the place I had hitherto known only as a departure point: for eighteen years from 1945 it had been the port at which I took the night-boat to Dublin, which reached the North Wall around seven next morning, in good time for catching the eight-something train from Westland Row station to Galway. Two or three times a year—never less than twice—the M.V. *Munster* or the M.V. *Leinster* from Liverpool Pier, for eighteen years. The boat-train from Euston, the Irish Mail, reached Liverpool at about nine in the evening—the line was not electrified then and the journey took four hours; there was then the short drive in the 'bus provided by the B. and I. Lines to take passengers from the train to the docks, putting off the Belfast passengers a little earlier, and the city of Liverpool was no more than the great Royal Liver Building on the waterfront, with its twin towers and its 'liver birds' with outstretched wings—sea gulls?—and massive black nineteenth-century civic buildings in the classical manner, and a glimpse of dingy streets, and the entrance to the Mersey Tunnel. Coming and going there was the view from the Mersey, the Liverpool skyline, with the Royal Liver Building in the foreground and the square tower of the Protestant cathedral in the background. I saw it all for the last time, and without regret, in 1963, when I sold the Connemara cottage and accepted, finally, that the long love-affair with Ireland was over. There is the 'death of the heart' with places no less than with people.

I had expected never to be in Liverpool again, and I hadn't wanted to return for this book, but my publisher had insisted on its importance. Liverpool, he had declared, had become a 'pretty important place in the last five years, the most swinging city in the country after London'; it was, he elaborated, the home of the Beatles, Cilla Black, and 'Z-Cars'. There were also two new cathedrals, one of them highly contemporary. I murmured that well, yes, I had thought I wouldn't mind seeing the new Roman Catholic cathedral.

'And the Cavern Club,' he said, sternly.

The Cavern Club? I groped around in the ragbag of my mind, at the bottom, where the oddments of 'with-it' general information are jumbled together. Wasn't that one of those teenager night-spots—a cellar, or something?

'It was where the Beatles started,' he explained, in the patient tone people of kind disposition use to foreigners and the not-very-bright.

The source of the Beatles? I was hoping to explore the source of the Thames, with which to conclude this book, but I was too old, I protested, to do the research in Liverpudlian night-life. And anyhow Nicholas Wollaston had covered all that in his admirable book, *Winter in England*, and pretty murky he had found it, what with the smoke and the din and the screaming.... We settled for the two cathedrals and a general daylight survey.

Mr. Wollaston, writing in 1965, did not find Liverpool a swinging city; he found it a 'kind of pre-Raphaelite city, left out in the rain and dirt when it should have been put behind glass', and a feeling of solid 'out-of-dateness', of nothing having happened, except the bombing, in fifty years. When he was there the first building of the great re-development scheme of the area facing Lime Street Station had only just begun;

when I was there two years later an immensely tall tower had arisen above the welter of scaffolding and cranes. I stood with my back to the imposing black buildings of libraries and museums in Brown Street and looked across to the gardens that descend from the back of the massive St. George's Hall to the Mersey Tunnel, and pondered what this lighthouse-like erection might be, rising above the Mersey; one of the new light-towers that were to replace lightships, I thought, having recently read about this in *The Times*. I consulted a policeman standing by a 'bus stop.

'That tall tower over there—is it some kind of a lighthouse?' My question seemed to astonish him.

'The tower? That's the city tower.' His tone conveyed that every person who was not mentally retarded knew *that*.

I murmured that I didn't know Liverpool, and he expanded: 'The new city precinct—that's the tower. There's going to be a revolving restaurant at the top.'

'Like the London post-office tower,' I said, brightly.

He swept that aside. 'Probably. What's going on here is a whole new civic centre—covered shopping centre, fly-over, pedestrian thoroughfares, seven pubs, two dance-halls, civic hall, the lot!'

'It'll be quite something!' I exclaimed, warmly, in an attempt to make up for previous dim-wittedness, and, taking what I hoped would seem an intelligent interest, 'When is it going to be finished?'

'Oh, God knows! Nineteen-something!'

'Before the end of the century, anyhow!'

I scribbled in my notebook about the seven pubs, etc., and after a moment he said, 'You can go and have a look. They've got a model of the whole thing over there.'

I thanked him and crossed the road to the gardens—St. John's Gardens—bright with beds of scarlet and pink geraniums, dingy with derelict-looking human beings slumped on every bench, and grotesque with more monuments of gentlemen in frock coats than I have ever seen assembled in one place. I threaded a way between the gaudy geraniums and the pompous statues and emerged into an area of narrow streets converging on to a market garden like Covent Garden, with, it seemed to me, the same names on the vans.

Hoardings enclosed the area at one side of the market, and the tower rose from a forest of cranes and scaffolding. It was difficult to tell what was demolition and what was new building, but a great deal was going on, with a great coming and going of heavy lorries, and a great rattling and banging and flying of white dust. The old Playhouse Theatre, brown and shabby, supported a notice saying that it was being re-developed. Round the corner from it was a plan in a glass case; I stopped before it and made some notes.

From this plan I learned that the new City Centre was called St. John's Precinct, and the tower St. John's Beacon, and that it was to be 450 feet high, with, as the policeman had said, a revolving restaurant; but he was wrong about the seven pubs, for itemised were 'five licensed premises', and not two dance-halls but a 'ballroom'. The area was to be a multi-level precinct with 150 shops and stores, air-conditioned pedestrian arcades, parking for 535 cars, a hotel, a retail market . . . altogether quite a place, as I had suggested to the policeman. Nearby was an office, with the model he had mentioned. I stood looking at it, and thinking of this modern phenomenon of building tall towers—the London post-office tower, and the even higher Cairo tower, in the Gazirah gardens across the Nile, with a revolving restaurant at the top, offering views as beautiful by night as by day, and the Tokyo tower, which the Japanese claim is the highest in the world—and of what Spengler had written years ago, in 1922, in his *Decline of the West*, about the 'demonic creations' of high buildings and tall towers presaging the decay of a civilisation, the final fling before destruction. In the Babylonian era they built the great *ziggurats*, the high, staged towers, such as are found at Ur-of-the-Chaldees, and elsewhere in Iraq. The legend of the Tower of Babel, which is universal, is one thing, but the origins of the tower exist in a temple among the ruins of Babylon, as I have seen. It is to be doubted whether the ruins of the modern Babylon will be as beautiful—and as enduring.

As with Coventry and Plymouth, a great part of the centre of Liverpool was destroyed during the Second World War by bombing, but unlike Coventry and Plymouth there was no immediate post-war reconstruction and in twenty years of inaction the city became seedy and rundown. The Special Redevelopment and Planning Committees of the early 'sixties gave it a new lease of life, 'taking Liverpool purposefully and efficiently into the twenty-first century', as John Willett puts it in his fine book about Liverpool, *Art in a City*.[1] Willett sees in the major planning operation which has been started, and which extends beyond the St. John's Precinct, the 'first outlines of a new city', and the 'hope of a transformation such as no other town in England has yet undergone'. What he calls the 'necropolis-like gardens' linking St. George's Hall—the law-courts—with the Mersey Tunnel are to be decked-over, to form 'what could well become one of the most handsome of Europe's great squares, with the hall itself restored to useful life as a place for national conferences'. By 1985 50,000 houses are to be cleared from behind the docks—the slum area—together with obsolete school buildings; a new motorway will bypass the City Centre; there will be increased pedestrian space and a new pattern of parks and green open spaces. By about 2015 Liverpool will be a new city, the project being expected to take not less than fifty years.

But long before then Liverpudlians will be able to dine at the top of the tower, like the Londoners, and the Egyptians, and shop in their new civic centre covered arcades, and feel themselves one up on Coventry—with whom there is a long-standing rivalry—because theirs are air-conditioned and

1. 1967.

covered, whereas Coventry's are neither.

There is a great deal that is drab and squalid in Liverpool, and some desperate slums, but there is also a great deal worth preserving, beginning with the handsome early nineteenth-century Customs House, with its cupola and classic pillared porch, and other nineteenth-century buildings in the grand classical manner—the grandest and most massive of which is St. George's Hall, with its terrific portico, with the equestrian statues of Queen Victoria and the Prince Consort in the open space in front, its broad flights of steps, and Trafalgar-Square-style bronze lions. The circular building of the Picton Library, across the road from it, is handsome, too, in the classical manner, with pillars; but the coal-black Walker Art Gallery next to it is another matter; there are seated figures of Michelangelo and Raphael at either side of the portico, and a figure representing Commerce at the top. The gallery was given by Sir Andrew Barclay Walker, brewer, mayor and patron of the arts, in the late nineteenth century. From its inception the gallery's policy has been one of middle-brow-ism, with the result, as Willett says, 'that few galleries have accumulated a larger number of valueless pictures'.

I had only time for a quick run-round during my visit; I was impressed by the handsomeness of the rooms, and oppressed by the number of Pre-Raphaelite paintings, which include the one Ruskin so much admired, by the Liverpool painter, W. L. Windus, *Burd Helen*, which depicts a knight on horseback and poor Helen on foot, holding her right hand to her side as though she had a stitch, and the horse already with its forelegs in the stream they are about to cross. Willett says it is the most famous nineteenth-century Liverpool painting, and calls Windus 'the one really notable painter' to come out of the Pre-Raphaelite-versus-foreign-painters squabble. I gazed at it with respect, but the Pre-Raphaelites are not for me; though neither were the abstract scrawls and daubs in the adjoining room, where a party of schoolboys were being, apparently, instructed in the appreciation of Modern Art.

It was a weekday afternoon and there were quite a number of people wandering through the galleries—though only the schoolboys contemplated the contemporary excesses.

Leaving the civic centre I went on up past the huge Adelphi Hotel—everything in Liverpool is huge—in search of what I most wanted to see, which was the Roman Catholic cathedral, the Cathedral of Christ the King.

In fact, no search is involved, for you can't, as they say, miss it. It is visible as the train comes into Lime Street Station, and it is visible from various parts of the city, set as it is on the low ridge that is the city's spine and rising like a lovely crown over Merseyside. You can take your bearings, too, if any are needed, from the square tower of the Anglican cathedral at the other end of the ridge.

Photographs do not do justice to this remarkable building which was completed in less than five years—begun in October, 1962, it was consecrated on May 14, 1967. It is not photogenic, and all the pictures make the wonderful lantern which is its crown look like a funnel; the edifice has to be seen entire, rising on its mound above the surrounding buildings, in the context of its setting, facing out across the city to the Mersey. It is revealed, then, as a modern building which is both beautiful and interesting. Had there been sufficient money at the end of the war to continue with Sir Edward Lutyen's grandiose scheme for a cathedral in the Romanesque style, Liverpool would have had an architectural monster at each end of Hope Street, for the great Gothic Anglican cathedral rises on its opposite mound only a short distance away, as oppressingly traditional as the Roman Catholic cathedral is excitingly contemporary.

For this Liverpool is indebted to Cardinal Heenan, who, as Archbishop of Liverpool, had the courage and the vision to abandon previous designs for the cathedral—one by Adrian Gilbert Scott followed the abandonment of the Lutyens design—

and seek for an appropriate design in the way that the design for Coventry Cathedral was sought—in the modern manner, through open competition.

The competition was announced in 1959, and the terms of it were not architecturally easy, for what the Archbishop and his advisers wanted was a cathedral to hold 3000 people, with the high altar visible to all, and none of them further from the sanctuary rails than seventy feet. There had to be a Lady Chapel, and a Blessed Sacrament Chapel, as well as other chapels, and a baptistry with a view of the high altar. Moreover, the completed Lutyens crypt had to be incorporated—and a large car park.

There were many entries, and the winner of the competition was Mr. Frederick Gibberd, who designed London Airport and Harlow New Town. Gibberd solved the problem of a vast congregation with a full view of the high altar, and not seated more than seventy feet from it, by siting it in the centre of a circular building. Thus the officiating priest stands in the midst of the people, a new pattern of worship in harmony with the ideas of liturgical reform of the Second Vatican Council.

The best approach to the cathedral is straight up Hope Street, passing the Philharmonic Hall on your right. You then receive the full impact of the dramatic effect of the square façade of the south porch, with the four electrically operated bells at the top, in a row, and dedicated to SS. Matthew, Mark, Luke and John. The evangelists are represented again in the winged emblems on the sliding doors, massively carved, and, to my mind, more suited to a Hindu temple or a Buddhist pagoda than an ultra-modern English cathedral in all other respects striking in its simplicity. The cross of Christ, flanked by the smaller crosses of the two thieves, is carved into the stonework of the façade below the belfry.

Through this strange, dramatic porch you come into what at first seems an even greater strangeness—a vast circular church dimly lit by blue light from tall, narrow blue glass windows. In the centre a rectangular block of marble on a flat circular plinth forms the high altar—druidical in its utter simplicity. Suspended as a canopy above it is a huge metal construction like a crown, and high above all this the great lantern of coloured glass designed by John Piper and Patrick Reyntiens, who were jointly responsible for the tremendous baptistry window of Coventry Cathedral, and here employ similar abstract ideas to represent the Holy Trinity, using all the colours of the spectrum, with bursts of white light. The seating sweeps round in a circle, sections of it kindled to crimson, other sections to gold, by the light poured down from above. The effect is dramatic and beautiful. The side chapels are plain and bare; the Stations of the Cross denoted by simple wooden crosses, the Confessionals unobtrusive. The chapel dedicated to St. George and the English Martyrs has windows by Piper and Reyntiens, and above it a gallery for television cameras.

There is a Chapel of St. Patrick, as might be expected in a cathedral in a city with so large an Irish community; there is a chapel of St. Thomas Aquinas, and a Chapel of St. Columba; none of these chapels were completed at the time of my visit. The Lady Chapel is the largest, and, after the Chapel of the Blessed Sacrament, the most beautiful. Its walls are lined with raw silk, a soft off-white, and a golden light from the narrow windows falls on the altar, as in the Chapel of the Blessed Sacrament. A sun-ray halo behind the small crucifix on the altar of the Lady Chapel is blue or gold according to the angle from which it is viewed, and the blue is repeated in the enamel on the stems of the six golden candlesticks. Behind the altar rises a tall Epstein-like Madonna and Child, designed by Robert Brumby. The tall straight figure of Our Lady stands with hands outstretched, meeting the outstretched hands of the Child Jesus standing in front of her. This is a ceramic statue, entirely modernistic, the figures formalised in straight lines, but conveys, nevertheless, a great feeling of maternal tenderness and childish innocence. That there is no other statue in the cathedral gives the right importance to this one, which is both beautiful and remarkable.

As in Coventry Cathedral the whole emphasis, religiously and aesthetically, is not on ornamentation but simplicity and symbolism.

A treasure of the cathedral is a beautifully carved metal holy water stoup, a gift from the Pope, to commemorate the dedication of the cathedral in 1967.

It is interesting that this Roman Catholic cathedral was designed by a Protestant, whilst the Anglican cathedral was designed by a Catholic. Cardinal Heenan finds in this a 'token of the growth of Christian Unity during this century', and in the opposing architectural trials of the two great churches, 'not a clash but a contrast'.

But the contrast is too much when going directly from one to the other. I found it, even, unbearable. The Anglican Cathedral Church of Christ is enormous, of red sandstone, and stands above a ravine rank with elders. The interior also is of sandstone, and the effect is almost frightening in its massive Gothic gloom. That, at least, was its effect on me, and even the elaborately carved and gilded high altar and reredos, which I suppose is very beautiful, in its richly ornate fashion, did not lessen it. The immense height of those dark red stone arches is overwhelmingly oppressive; the effect is of vast brickwork rising in monstrous height to the darkness of arched upper galleries and the immensity of the roof. Only the Lady Chapel escapes this sombreness. As with the Lady Chapel of Ely Cathedral, it is separate from the main cathedral, like an independent church, and it is light and feminine, with a fine east window, a blue and gold reredos, and a graceful vaulted ceiling.

In the main cathedral I liked a conventional group of statuary, of the Holy Family, at the west end, where work is still in progress. As a work of art it is of probably no great importance, but I liked its quality of tenderness, and its realism which escaped sentimentality. I inquired about it and learned that it was acquired about five years ago, and that the sculptor was a woman, Josephina di Vasconcelles. The group had not been originally designed for the cathedral, and in its gentle greyness it does not 'belong' in that vast, dark Gothic place, but I left with a feeling of something like gratitude that it was there, something moving and human, and of human dimension. . . .

From the top of the broad flight of steps leading up to the porch there is a view out over the houses to the Mersey—a notice says to close the side door by which one enters because of the strong winds. I stood on these steps with my daughter, just over thirty years ago when we took time off on our return from the Dublin Horse Show to go and see 'the new cathedral'. All I remembered was that it was very big, and very unfinished. Yet the foundation stone was laid as far back as 1904, by Edward VII. The completion of the Lady Chapel was the first objective, and this was consecrated in 1910. The cathedral itself was not consecrated until 1924. In the year in which the Lady Chapel was completed the architect changed his plans for the main structure, which he had originally designed to have twin towers. World War I was a setback, but work on the cathedral never entirely ceased, and by 1920 operations were in full swing, making the consecration possible four years later, just twenty years after the foundation stone was laid. The Reverend Canon Dillistone, formerly Dean of Liverpool, writes[1] that 'it was the first time in England that a cathedral had been consecrated on a wholly new site since the thirteenth century. King George V and Queen Mary were present together with no less than eight Archbishops with forty-five Bishops representing the world-wide Anglican Communion.'

From then until the outbreak of World War II was a crucial time, but in 1934 Lord Vestey, and his brother, Sir Edmund

1. *The Pictorial History of Liverpool Cathedral*, Pitkin Pictorials, 1965.

Vestey, with a 'munificent gift' made it possible for the great tower—known as the Vestey tower—to be put in hand. 'Progress in the years preceding the Second World War was eminently satisfactory,' says the Canon, 'and in June, 1939, more than 250 men were at work on the site.' But the war was a second setback; bomb blast blew out the windows of the Lady Chapel and the south wall of the choir, and it was not until Christmas Day, 1955, that the chapel could be used again. Nevertheless the work did to some extent go on during the war years, and the huge central section of the cathedral was brought into use in July, 1941, only two months after the biggest air attack on Liverpool. By 1954 funds were exhausted and a new appeal was issued—and generously met. By the end of 1959 over two and a half million pounds had been spent. Will it ever be finished? In the summer of 1967 the work in progress on the west wall did appear to be the completion of the task begun over sixty years ago.

Just as across the road from the huge Roman Catholic church in Norwich there is a synagogue, so opposite this vast Anglican cathedral in Liverpool there is an Islamic centre, with the name of the *imām* over the door. It stands at the end of a terrace of decaying houses, some with their windows already boarded-up, pending demolition.

I strolled back to the City Centre, passing on the way an antique shop which displayed in the front of its window a crudely coloured print of two Oriental-looking girls in old-fashioned bathing suits, with the caption: *Come to sunny Liverpool for your holidays*!

I came into the shopping thoroughfare of Ranelagh Street, with Lewis's new building on the corner, its entrance porch surmounted by a nude bronze male figure which I thought had an Epstein look about it. From Mr. Willett's book I learned later that it is in fact by Epstein, and represents *The Spirit of Liverpool Resurgent*. Mr. Willett concedes that commissioning Epstein was a bold effort, but considers the figure badly placed, and 'one of Epstein's less successful works'. He considers, also, that 'the immediate focussing of the spectator's attention on the figure's genitals has remained distracting to the citizens, so that the three smaller but more impressive relief panels beneath it go largely unobserved'. Well, I don't know. It's true I did not observe, except vaguely, the panels over the doors, but I think I would not have observed them even if the figure had not been there, perched high above. Is anyone, in this day and age, 'distracted' by genitals?

I noticed, as I walked along, *A Man for All Seasons* showing at a cinema, Billy Graham coming to the Central Hall, Peter Robinson's closing down, *Hedda Gabler* on at the theatre in Hope Street, and 'Folk at the Phil.' A great deal goes on in Hope Street, which has the Cathedral of Christ the King at one end and the ravine above which rises the Anglican cathedral at the other. It is the central section of the ridge, and not only has it the fine building of the Philharmonic Hall—where a lot goes on, not least the Royal Liverpool Philharmonic Orchestra—but also the College of Art, and the modern block of the Design Centre, with its elaborately carved murals by William Mitchell —who did the sliding doors of the south porch of Christ the King—and the University Schools of Architecture and Civic Design (the university itself is at the other end, close to the cathedral). There is a terrace of attractive though rundown early nineteenth-century houses, and the area is by way of being an artists' quarter.

A lot goes on in Liverpool generally, apart from its life as a great seaport and commercial centre; it has a number of active and extremely modern artists and poets; it has its own annual Academy Exhibition, and what would appear to be a quite aggressive cultural energy. It is the home not merely of the Beatles but of one of the finest orchestras in the country; it produces novelists, singers, guitarists, footballers, sculptors; and its tremendous city redevelopment scheme does undoubtedly represent a Merseyside renaissance.

I had revisited Liverpool interested only in the two cathe-drals; I left interested in the city itself, excited not only by the imaginative modernity of the Roman Catholic cathedral, but by the sense of *happening*. It is something you feel strongly in Coventry, but Liverpool no longer has to be jealous of Coventry—or touchy about Manchester. When they come to rebuild Ranelagh Street they can no doubt find a more suitable —and a worthier—place for the Epstein sculpture of *Liverpool Resurgent*—down on the waterfront, perhaps, like Zadkine's stirring sculpture, *The Destroyed City*, on the Rotterdam waterfront, or in one of the new parks that are part of the redevelopment scheme, but in their new and shining city they should keep at least one of the coal-black nineteenth-century classical buildings to show what England's second city once was.

15

Plymouth, Doubly Elizabethan

FROM the first Queen Elizabeth to the second, from Sir Francis Drake sailing from Plymouth in 1577 to 'circumnavigate the globe', to Sir Francis Chichester in 1967 beginning and ending there his single-handed voyage round the world, the Devon seaport at the head of Plymouth Sound may be said to be doubly Elizabethan.

I wanted it for this book because it is so essentially a part of English history, like Greenwich, and because, like Coventry, it is in a sense a new city, having been largely rebuilt since it was laid waste in 1941. I wanted to see the new Plymouth, the post-Second-World-War Plymouth of the reigning Elizabeth, and the old Plymouth of the first Elizabeth, which suffered little damage in the blitz.

I was fortunate in having as my guide to Plymouth my daughter, Jean, who has lived in south Devon since 1945, and who knows and likes this city. One of her reasons for liking it is because it is, as she says, a 'real' place, which is a reason I appreciate, being myself addicted to places in which the natives predominate and not the retired middle-class from outside, towns and villages which are not show-places milling with tourists, like Stratford-upon-Avon, or chronically 'picturesque', like Rye in Sussex, and Broadway in the Cotswolds, but where ordinary people live and work and have their being, taking the ancient monuments and historic landmarks for granted.

The naturalness of Plymouth was quick to assert itself. When we turned out of the rebuilt railway station, with its modern block of offices built over it, and went on up past a terrace of shabby, decaying houses, with peeling plaster and neglected front gardens, to a nondescript area called Western Approach, there was suddenly a familar smell.

'Pooh!' I exclaimed. 'Fish-and-chips!'

Jean said, serenely, 'I told you—this is a real place.'

We crossed a road and passed a piece of wasteland being used as a car park and came to the top of a broad open space descending in terraces of lawns and flower-beds—Armada Way. There were flowering lilac bushes, ornamental cherry trees still with traces of blossom, the scarlet, crimson and gold of tulips and wallflowers, and, as we descended, a pool with a fountain on a flagged terrace, and, nearby, tables marked out for chess or draughts. Modern buildings flank Armada Way at a discreet distance; an office block is called Mayflower House. At the bottom of Armada Way, where it meets the wide shopping thoroughfare of Royal Parade, there is the monument known as Drake's Drum, the design for which was based on the original drum; the monument commemorates the rebuilding of the City Centre in 1947. The plan for the rebuilding was 'to make new Plymouth as modern as possible, but to keep old Plymouth as antique as is compatible with practical use and sanitariness.'[1]

The beginning of the reconstruction of the city was marked by a foundation stone laid by George VI near the then ruined Guildhall. The Guildhall, of which the tower survived the bombing, has been rebuilt in the same Victorian style and is handsome enough in its way, but dwarfed by all the high modern buildings of the area. There is a skyscraper here, sixteen storeys, from the covered top of which—they call it the roof-deck—there is a fine view out over the sprawling 'Three

1. J. P. Watson and P. Abercrombie, *A Plan for Plymouth*, 1943.

Towns' which comprise Plymouth, the borough of Devonport and the township of East Stonehouse having been combined with Plymouth in 1914. The geography of the waterfront is also clearly to be made out from this roof-deck—which is, in fact, singularly reminiscent of the deck of a ship; the two inlets into Plymouth Sound are to be seen, the Cattewater to the east, and Hamaoze to the west, both flanked by high ground on which there are forts. On the northern side of the entrance to the Cattewater is the Royal Citadel of Charles II. The other way stretches the broad green promenade of the famous Hoe, extending along the Sound, with Drake's Island, formerly St. Nicholas, off-shore, facing across to Cornwall—there is some uncertainty as to why it is called Drake's Island, and a map dated as late as 1850 shows it as St. Nicholas Island. The Devonport dockyard fronts the Hamoaze inlet, and Stonehouse is in between. Church towers and spires thrust up from the sprawling, misty panorama, together with the tall blocks and towers of modern buildings, all merging into a confusing, far-flung sprawl.

But down below, and continuing on up and over the grassy slopes to the Hoe, it all seems much easier; there is, after all, no need to struggle out to the docks; Devonport and Stone-house had their day during the Regency period, and some good Regency building remains, but we are concerned with the Plymouth of the two Elizabeths, and when we come out on to the promenade of the Hoe we have the two eras most ad-mirably combined, for here is where Drake played that tra-ditional—or legendary?—game of bowls whilst the Spanish Armada loomed up, and here is his statue looking out to sea, and here, also, is a ladies' bowling match in progress, the ladies in their white sweaters and blouses as nonchalant under the gaze of the onlookers at the other side of the hedge as Drake is reported to have been before the advance of the Spanish galleons.

There is a handsome naval war memorial up here, and

across from it the upper part of the original Eddystone light-house, rebuilt by John Smeaton in 1759; when a new light-house was constructed part of the Smeaton lighthouse was brought ashore and re-erected on the Hoe as a Trinity House landmark, in 1822. The view out over the Sound, looking across to Cornwall, is very beautiful. Charles II is said to have gone into raptures about it; he was, indeed, so charmed that he built a house within the Citadel for his use when he visited Plymouth, which, apparently, he did frequently. The fourth Eddystone lighthouse is fourteen miles out to sea and hardly to be seen in daylight, but the famous breakwater which protects the Sound, and which is a remarkable piece of nineteenth-century civil engineering, is visible two miles south of the Hoe; behind it large liners and merchant ships can shelter in deep water. It is almost a mile long, and lighted at the west end by a lighthouse and at the east end by a beacon.

It would have been pleasant to have strolled along the Hoe in the warm May sunshine, but old Plymouth lies in the other direction, and after lingering for a few moments looking down on the children splashing in the shallow water of a swimming pool on a beach we turned our backs on the Hoe and set off down the hill to the old harbour, the Barbican, with the Citadel on its low grassy hill above us on the left. The road dips down past the Dolphin Inn, where the Tolpuddle Martyrs were first lodged on their return from transportation to Australia; there is a plaque on the wall of the Barbican to commemorate the return of the four of them. They were, it will be recalled, six Dorset farm labourers exiled for attempting to organise village trade unions, though officially their crime was 'admini-stering an illegal oath'; they were sentenced in 1834 to seven years' exile, but as a result of public agitation they were given a free pardon in 1836. The plaque was presented by trade unions and bears the words: *Justice was their cause.*

A monument in the form of a small arch commemorates the sailing of the *Mayflower* from the pier there in 1620, with a plaque presented in 1891 by descendants and relatives of the Pilgrim Fathers.

Another plaque commemorates the *Sea Venture*, in which Sir George Somers was leading an expedition from Plymouth to Virginia in 1609, but which was wrecked on a reef in the Bermudas, or Somers Islands, as they came to be called. The survivors reached the main island, then uninhabited, and were the first colonists of England's oldest colony, which received its charter from the Virginia company in 1612, when Somers, returning to it from Virginia, for 'victuals', died there.

There are other plaques along the Barbican walls, but, oddly, nothing about Drake; but then his statue is up on the Hoe, and in a sense all Plymouth is his memorial.

After a visit to a pleasant old waterside inn we sat on the steps of the pier from which the *Mayflower* had sailed to eat our sandwiches, and we thought about the people who had set out for the New World in that small sailing ship—it was only 180 tons—with a hundred passengers crowded on board. They left Plymouth on September 6, 1620, and stepped ashore at the other side of the Atlantic on December 21 of that year, to form the colony which was to become Plymouth, Massachusetts, thirty-seven miles south-east of Boston. In that first terrible winter half of them died; corn was planted on their levelled graves in the spring, so that the hostile Indians would not know how decimated were their numbers.

Across the road from the quayside three capstans lean out from a narrow cobbled pavement above the roadway, relics of the days when the waters of the Sound were very much further in, laving the base of Citadel Hill, as shown in an early eighteenth-century print. Here is Mayflower House, at which the Pilgrim Fathers slept the night before they sailed; it is now a shop for curios from old ships. A plaque on the wall sets forth the names of the Pilgrim Fathers and their occupations—silk worker, of London, wool carder, coppersmith, sawyer, merchant, servant-boy, to name a few. It is interesting that no women are mentioned; there is not even an 'and wife'. The women shared the hardships with the men, both aboard ship and in those pioneer days in the New World; there should surely have been some mention of them on the roll of honour.

Close by is New Street, which was new in the sixteenth century, when a merchant called John Sparke was mayor of Plymouth for the first time in 1583. The Sparke family were what nowadays would be called 'developers'. They bought up old properties and demolished them and built new properties on the site. One of the properties the Sparkes bought after the Dissolution was the Friary of the Carmelites, but this John Sparke kept to live in himself; the site is now Plymouth's Friary station. New Street was one of Mayor Sparke's developments in 1584—'Sparke's new streate . . . paved, leading towards the new key.' The 'new key' is what is now known as the Barbican, or watergate; but the new quay was pre-Sparke, having been built in 1572.

Several of Sparke's houses still stand in New Street today. Number 32 was bought by the Old Plymouth Society in 1926, when it was in ruins; the Society restored it and presented it to the city, and is now trying to restore other Elizabethan houses in the street. Number 32 is open to the public without charge. It is typical of the period, timbered and gabled, with mullioned windows spanning the breadth of the front—to secure the maximum of light from the narrow street—and the walls are of limestone. Inside, the ceilings are supported by heavy oak beams, and the floors are of narrow planks. The rooms have been furnished with period furniture—there is a bedroom, with four-poster bed, a living room, a kitchen with utensils.

In an excellent booklet available at Number 32 the writer of it, Crispin Gill, suggests that the shipwrights who built the ships on the beaches 'were no doubt the same craftsmen who put the woodwork in the new houses. They used the same oak, and carved it in their rough style where it was wanted; they panelled the rooms just as they panelled the captains' cabins aboard the ships they built.' There are specimens of this carving in the house. Sparke's new houses were built for the sea-captains and merchants of the town, who liked to have good houses near the quay. The really wealthy people, the Quality, lived at the other side of the town.

At the back of Number 32 there is a small paved courtyard, and the structure of the house at the back, with two gables forming a V, and windows facing each other at each side of the V so closely that it would be easily possible to lean out and shake hands, is curiously and interestingly echoed in the design of the recently built three-storey row of flats at the end of New Street. This modern building is a striking example of how old and new domestic architecture may be harmonised. There are still in New Street some of the warehouses which began to be built there early in the nineteenth century, when the street had come down in the world, and the merchants had moved up to the Hoe and out to the new suburbs. Small houses began to be built round the capacious old ones, and the old houses became rack-rented and slummified; the cottages built in back gardens for servants were still occupied by the 'lower orders', but the masters had moved themselves and their servants and apprentices away from what had become the squalor of the harbour area.

Crispin Gill mentions a letter written by Drake in 1594 praising Sparke, who was a friend of his, for his work for the town. Drake was himself Mayor of Plymouth for those few peaceful years ashore before he went off on that last expedition in 1596 from which he was fated not to return. His piracies filled the exchequer of Elizabeth I, and enabled him to buy Buckland Abbey, in Devon, from his share of the spoils—it is now a Drake museum—but the one really admirable thing he did in his short life (he died in his middle fifties) was organising a new water-supply for Plymouth. . . .

Turning right at the end of New Street one comes quickly to Hoe Gate Street, where there are more sixteenth-century houses of stone and timber, though not as good as in New Street. The Hoe Gate of the walled town stood here; a plaque gives the information that it was rebuilt in 1657, sold in 1695, and finally removed in 1863. There are other streets in which Elizabethan houses still stand—some buried under modern plaster—notably Looe Street, Notte Street, and Southside Street; the latter is first mentioned in 1591.

From the top of Hoe Gate Street a short walk up some grassy slopes leads to the massive, baroque main gate of the Citadel, designed by Sir Thomas Fitz in 1670, and not by Sir Christopher Wren as believed until the Wren Society declared for Fitz in the nineteenth volume of its publication. There is not, really, much of interest once you have passed in under this ornate portal. Turning to the right you may walk for some distance along the ramparts, on which ancient cannon are mounted, and descend near the Royal Chapel of St. Katherine-upon-the-Hoe. Of the various buildings shown in the eighteenth-century print referred to earlier only four remain: the Guard House, now the Guard Room of the Royal Artillery garrison; the Governor's House, rebuilt for the second time in 1903, and now the H.Q. offices; the Storehouse, converted in 1844 into a barrack block, and the Royal Chapel. The original front door of the Governor's House, of massive oak, and iron-studded, is now the front door of the R.A. mess. Part of the old ramparts were lost when the New Block, known as 'B' Block, was built in 1897. Charles II had the Citadel built partly as a protection against the Dutch fleet, but also to keep in order the Cromwellian city that had successfully withstood the Royalist two years' siege. Work began on it in 1666, and it was finished in 1671. The ramparts were originally surrounded by a deep moat, the drawbridge for which was in front of the main gate, but this was removed in 1888 and the moat filled in, and now only the chains of the portcullis remain.

Drake began building a fort on the site after the defeat of the

Spanish Armada, for the defence of the town and the annoyance of the enemy, as he said in his petition to the Queen. It was to be triangular in design with a broad base towards the sea; that was in 1558; there was a query about it in 1594, and as late as 1624, twenty-eight years after Drake's death, it was still not completed, and in 1666 it was demolished and work on the Royal Citadel began.

I could not find much interest in the Royal Chapel. That it stands upon a site of a former chapel of the fourteenth century, and that at the time of Drake it became a 'garrison church', which it still is, does not alter the fact that it was extensively altered in 1845, and it is the nineteenth century which predominates today. Across from it, facing the officers' mess, there is an extraordinary statue of George II wearing what would appear to be a Roman toga and a crown of laurels. It was put up by Robert Pitt in 1728, 'at the expense of Louis du Tour, an Officer of the Garrison, to mark His Majesty's ascension to the throne in 1727'. It stood, then, in the middle of the square, but was moved to its present position in 1948, the year in which it was repaired after war-damage in 1941. It stands, now, with its back to the chapel, and flanked by cannon on two sides.

When we were leaving the Citadel the guide at the main gate greeted us friendlily, as when we went in, and inquired whether we had seen the Chapel, which he had recommended to us, and when we assured him that we had, asked what we were going to do next.

'Go home,' I said.

'Have you seen Drake's church?' he asked quickly, and before we could reply was pointing it out just down below— the tall Perpendicular tower, the three long roofs. 'You shouldn't miss that,' he urged. 'The largest church in Devon!'

We thanked him and made our way the short distance to it. It is, in fact, the largest parish church in the West Country, and, in the words of Professor Nikolaus Pevenser, 'a typical example of the main church of a thriving fifteenth-century town'.

The oldest part of the church dates from the end of the fourteenth century, and the history of the church is interesting, being, in a sense, the history of Plymouth. There is record of a church on the site as early as the Norman Conquest, when Plymouth was a small fishing village known as South Town or Sutton, and St. Andrew's was a chapel served by the Augustinian Priory of Plympton. The early vicars were appointed from the Priory; the first officiated during the reign of William Rufus. St. Andrew's is mentioned in a survey of the Western Churches of the Kingdom made by order of Pope Nicholas in 1291.

By 1377 the fishing village of Sutton had become the fourth largest town in the Kingdom—the other three being London, York, and Bristol—and the church grew with it. The South Chancel Aisle, then known as the Chapel of St. Mary, was built by the great church builder, John Edenes, in 1380. In 1439 the growing town received its charter and became Plymouth, and in 1440 work began in earnest to build a great church worthy of the town. Twenty years later a Plymouth merchant called Thomas Yogge, who had the distinction of being three times mayor, paid for the building of the tower, on condition that the townsfolk should supply the 'stuffe', that is to say the materials. The interior of the church suffered during the Reformation, and again during the restoration carried out in the early nineteenth century, when much of the woodwork was destroyed, including the finely carved screen. The church was again restored in 1874-5, by Sir Gilbert Scott, but was this time improved by the abolition of galleries and high pews, and by the opening up of the tower arch. A third and vastly more major restoration was carried out in 1949, when rebuilding was begun after destruction by incendiaries in March, 1941, when the interior was gutted, all that was left being the walls, the Tower, and the pillars. Later the shell was laid out with lawns and flowers and for some years was known as the Garden Church, and as in the ruins of the old Coventry Cathedral, services were held from time to time. On St. Andrew's Day, November 30, 1957, the church was reconsecrated by the Bishop of Exeter, assisted by the Bishops of Plymouth and Liverpool.

But to go back in history, linking the church with the history of Plymouth: on October 2, 1501, Catherine of Aragon arrived at Plymouth from Spain, to marry the eldest son of Henry VII, Prince Arthur. To give thanks for her safe arrival after a rough voyage she went in procession to St. Andrew's. The cardinal who arranged her marriage, Adrian de Castello, later became vicar. The rest of poor Catherine's story, as the first wife of her brother-in-law, after he became Henry VIII, does not belong here, but it is of some interest that Cattewater was named after her—Catherine water.

As I write this there is great excitement over the return of Sir Francis Chichester to Plymouth from his epic voyage, and it is therefore interesting to recall the excitement that Sunday morning of August 9, 1573, when Captain Francis Drake sailed into Plymouth after his Nombre de Dios exploit in July the previous year. Everybody was in church, including the Mayor and Corporation, whose custom it was to walk in procession from the Guildhall down by the harbour up to St. Andrew's. Drake's wife, also, was in the church, and the sermon was in progress, when the great news of the captain's return was 'brought unto his family', and this 'did so speedily passe all over the church, and surpasse their minds with desire and delight to see him, that few or none remained with the preacher, all hastening to see the evidence of God's love and blessing towards our Gracious Queen and country, by the fruite of our Captain's labour and success'. Seven years later he again sailed into Plymouth Sound, this time after circumnavigating the globe. In St. Andrew's there is a primitive scratching on a window-sill in the south aisle which is known as the Drake Crest. It is believed to be sixteenth century and to have been done with the tip of a mason's trowel; the scratching shows a ship, presumably the *Golden Hind*, with a cord from its bows encircling a globe. Drake returned to Plymouth on November 30, 1580, and on April 4 the Queen knighted him aboard his ship at Deptford; his coat of arms consisted of a ship surmounting a globe, from the bow a cord drawn round the world, and in the top left-hand corner symbolically the hand of God guiding the ship; below this, a visor and a shield. The scratching in the church is therefore a part of the crest.

Drake always worshipped in St. Andrews when he was in Plymouth, and the burial register shows the burial of his wife there. She died in 1583; he married again two years later. There is a complete set of baptismal, marriage and burial registers, dating from 1581, and English history is embedded in them. An interesting baptismal record is of a son to Frances and James Bligh, christened William, in the parish church of St. Andrew's; he was to become Captain Bligh of the *Bounty*. Another interesting baptismal entry is of the rabbi in Plymouth, who on June 22, 1825, was baptised a Christian. He was later to become the first Anglican bishop in Jerusalem.[1] Two of Sir John Hawkins' children were baptised there, and the entrails of Sir Martin Frobisher and of Admiral Blake were interred there, Frobisher's corpse being 'carried home to be buried in London', and Blake's 'at Westminster among ye kings'.

In 1620 the Pilgrim Fathers gathered in St. Andrew's to renew their Solemn League and Covenant before sailing, and during the long royalist siege of the Civil War the citizens of Plymouth, the city's gates closed against the king, met in St. Andrew's for mutual comfort and the reaffirmation of their Cromwellian faith.

Then the twentieth century and the chapter of history which was the Second World War, and a great part of the ancient city of Plymouth became a rubble heap, and its fine old parish church a hollow shell; but over the north door a single word was inscribed on a board: *Resurgam*. The creation of the Garden Church in the ruins was an expression of that determination to

1. Bishop Solomon Alexander.

rise again, and, as we have seen, in 1949 the great work was begun, and within eight years a truly wonderful piece of restoration was carried out, under the direction of Mr. Frederick Etchells, F.R.I.B.A. The church as it stands today is, as the Vicar, the Reverend John Cavell, put it to me, 'The original church but with a new roof and a new "inside".' Though, to be sure, the lofty and beautiful mediaeval pillars remain; work on them was the first part of the restoration.

A feature of the mediaeval church was the remarkable 'wagon roof', which consisted of barrel vaulting; in the reconstruction this has been contrived by means of concrete vaults with oak ribs, achieving the same effect. This year, the Vicar tells me, sixty-one coloured ceiling bosses have been placed in the roof, replacing the mediaeval ones destroyed in the blitz. They are made of fibre-glass and are three-dimensional, and tell the story of Plymouth through 900 years. The boss for today is of *Gipsy Moth IV* and her heroic master, designed to 'symbolise the spirit of man in our time'.

But remarkable as this ceiling is, the great glory of the restored church is the stained glass by John Piper in the east end, and in the tower, at the west end. These windows are of a quite startling beauty. The east end of the church was always considered very fine, but it can surely never have been more beautiful than now. Like the wonderful Piper baptistry window in Coventry Cathedral these windows in St. Andrew's, Plymouth, have an almost indescribable richness of colour. There are three windows in the east end, simple and direct in their biblical pictorial statement. The Astor Memorial Window in the Tower, dedicated to the second Viscount Astor, Mayor of Plymouth 1939–44, is not so much abstract as complicated in its symbolism, which concerns itself with the Instruments of the Passion, the Crown of Thorns, the Crowing Cock, the Thirty Pieces of Silver, and so forth. The note of explanation given in the excellent guide to the church[1] is worth quoting: 'The

1. By Michael T. Fermer and John F. Parkinson, 1958. Reprinted 1967.

Instruments of the Passion have been represented since the thirteenth century. They—or some of them—appear in many mediaeval churches, and they have been rather more commonly used by craftsmen in the West Country than anywhere else since the fifteenth century. They appear carved on capitals, bench-ends, roof-bosses, and in stained glass. In the design,' the authors continue, 'the Ladder and the Reed and Spear form a St. Andrew's Cross in honour of the dedication of the church. In the tracery lights at the top of the window are shown the Sun and Moon in Eclipse, and the Sponge moistened with vinegar.'

This window is ten years old, which means that it is 'pre-Coventry'. The three wonderful windows at the east end were put in only in 1966. There are two more to come, as I write this, to go in the east windows of the two transepts, in the summer of this year, 1967.

It was tremendously exciting to enter that long nave, nobly flanked by the beautiful grey Perpendicular arches, and experience the sudden confrontation of that blaze of glory—for it is nothing less.

The church has great treasures in the form of sixteenth- and seventeenth-century Communion plate, pieces of great interest and beauty, but what makes the church exciting and stimulating are the twentieth-century contributions to its re-creation —the wonderful Piper windows, the remarkable ceiling bosses, the striking modern altar ornaments and frontals. In this church as in the new Coventry Cathedral the historic past and the living present meet and merge.

There was no time to go out to Stonehouse after that, and I personally had no wish to, though my daughter regretted the omission, feeling that I was missing something important, but I was concerned with *Elizabethan* Plymouth, past and present, and for me the Plymouth pilgimage ended most fittingly there at Drake's church, facing one way to the sixteenth-century harbour and the other to the mid-twentieth-century City Centre.

16

Thames Head

WITH so much about the Thames as 'London's river' at the beginning of this book it seemed somehow right and proper to end with Thames Head, now officially accepted by the Thames Conservancy board, and by people who know about rivers and are called potamologists, as the authentic source of the Thames. For anyone proposing to make the journey by train it is not easy; Cirencester is the nearest town and it is no longer on the railway; the train goes no farther than Swindon, from which it is an hour's 'bus journey to Cirencester, by an hourly service. Thames Head is then three miles from Cirencester, which is under an hour's walk, but the meadow in which the river rises is not easy to find, being down an unmarked lane and across a wide field and along a rough muddy track, to an old ash tree leaning out across a heap of stones up through which bubbles the spring which is the source—except on those days when, inexplicably—to anyone but a potamologist—there is no water there at all.

Endeavouring to work out trains and 'buses, it seemed quite an expedition, and it was a relief when Gilbert Turner said firmly, 'You'd never find it! You'd better let me take you by car.'

This made it possible to plot a course through the Thames valley and take in a number of attractive places on the river or its tributaries.

It was June by then and the white hawthorn along the motor-roads was going over, yielding to the red, and there was pink chestnut blossom everywhere. There could be no lovelier time of year for going in search of the source of the Thames.

Out again, then, along the M.4, and nothing of interest, except the shadowy hulk of Windsor Castle away over to the left, misty in the morning haze, and a lovely shallow valley in the Chilterns, called Bix Bottom, remarkably unchanged since I last saw it some thirty years ago, and a pleasant village called Nettlebed, and then Dorchester-on-Thames; the River Thame, the tributary which joins the Thames there, is crossed before reaching the town, and is a small sylvan stream.

But there is nothing sylvan about the non-stop stream of traffic that hurtles along Dorchester's old-world High Street which has the misfortune to be the Oxford road; a by-pass is called for, so that those who wish to cross the road to visit the historic Abbey do not do so at risk of their lives. Dorchester is quite chronically picturesque, with every other sixteenth-, seventeenth- or eighteenth-century house an antique shop, and with inns to match, but the Abbey church of SS. Peter and Paul and Birinus, lying back among trees across that perilous road, and approached through a lych gate, is most noble, and, in its austere beauty, aloof from the twentieth-century racket. It is now the parish church of Dorchester, rebuilt on the site of the Saxon cathedral, which was given to the Augustinian order at the time of the Norman Conquest, when the see of Dorchester was moved to Lincoln, then a more flourishing town. The first bishop was Birinus, a Benedictine monk of Rome, who, sent on a proselytising mission by the Pope, landed in Wessex in 634, converted the king, Cynegils, and founded the see of Dorchester.

The church represents every century since the Conquest. The south-west aisle was built in the fourteenth century for the parishioners, who had hitherto been allowed the use of the Norman nave of the monastic church, but this arrangement

o

had led to friction between the townsfolk and the community, so a separate church was built, although part of the Abbey Church. The fine Norman nave still exists; the long stretch of wall is probably Saxon, and it is believed that the south walk of the Cloister was built against it in the twelfth century.

'We notice,' the Reverend Harold Best, the present Vicar, points out, in a brochure available at the church, 'a blocked up doorway which led from the Nave into the Cloister, made when the windows above were constructed.' He adds that the stone coffins to be found there are Saxon and were dug up in the churchyard. There is a great deal of medieval glass; the east window is made up of fourteenth-century glass collected from other windows in the abbey when repairs to windows were being carried out in the eighteenth century. Even older glass is in the south wall, where there are thirteenth-century panels depicting scenes from the life of St. Birinus and possibly taken from the Norman east window.

But the great mediaeval treasure is the Jesse Window, representing the genealogical tree of Jesus. The tree grows out of the recumbent stone figure of Jesse on the window-sill, and within the panels formed by the stone tracery of the branches are depicted kings and prophets from the Old Testament. Damage was done to the window by the Cromwellians, who smashed the figure of the Virgin and Child, and figures of Christ at the top, but figures of the Wise Men and the Angel Gabriel may still be made out. The glass is pale, like much mediaeval glass, but of immense interest and a sad beauty.

St. Birinus has a secluded little chapel and a modern shrine; the shrine is a little garish in the general monastic bareness of the church. The tomb of the Crusader, Sir John Holcomb, one of three tombs below the altar steps, is very striking, and is considered a magnificent piece of mediaeval carving, and 'one of the most impressive effigies in this country'. On all the effigies are traces of the original colouring.

The Norman font is very remarkable and very beautiful, being of lead, with figures of the apostles in relief; its stone base was provided in 1835, when restoration of the church began. Many of the Abbey treasures were destroyed at the Reformation, but the font escaped.

There is a beautiful cloister garden, which until recently was part of the vicarage grounds and used for grazing the Vicar's cows, but, says the Vicar, 'through the generosity of many American friends and a local garden committee this has been laid out and visitors are welcome to picnic here and enjoy its peace and seclusion'.

I liked very much a notice in the church porch: *Music in the Abbey; Flowers by Candlelight; Wine and Cheese in the Vicarage Gardens.*

Wine and cheese, and music and flowers, in such a setting, is an idea of which the Augustinian monks would themselves have approved, I thought, as we went back through the lych gate and across the churchyard to the twentieth-century road rip-roaring on its way to Oxford—that seat of learning and of the motor industry.

Through the pleasant old town of Abingdon, then, in Berkshire, with narrow crowded shopping streets and a market cross and unattractive outskirts, and on to Faringdon, with a Norman church and grey stone buildings, and at the entrance to a secondary road a notice: Road unsuitable for vehicles of the *Queen Mary* type.

Not being of the *Queen Mary* type we turned into it, with lush meadows on either side, white with daisies, golden with buttercups. It was lovely, gentle, undulating country, very English, and because we were heading for Kelmscott, by what Mackail in his *Life of William Morris* called one of the 'back ways of approaching it', some lines from *The Earthly Paradise*, which I have remembered from early youth, came into my mind:

O June, O June, that we desired so,
Wilt thou not make us happy on this day?

I was brought up by a socialist father—there were real
socialists in those days—to revere William Morris; Bob Mannin
was one of the young socialists who used to go to Morris's
house at Hammersmith, and were all their lives, I suppose,
proud of the memory; certainly my father was. All my life I
had known about the Kelmscott Press, but only now, so late in
the day, was I seeing Kelmscott Manor, Morris's most beautiful, and most loved home. Morris approached Kelmscott, in
1871, by what Mackail called the 'grand entry', by boat up the
'lovely lonely waterway', a thirty-mile journey from Oxford.
Morris described the journey in the poem I had remembered;
it was in June he came to the house, and he also wrote lyrically
of it in prose—of the hawthorn and wild roses in the lanes by
which the house was approached, of entering through a door
in the wall, and of the garden 'redolent of the June flowers', of
the roses 'rolling over one another', and of the blackbirds, and
the rooks in the high elms, and he felt that 'the house itself was
a fit guardian for all the beauty of this heart of summer'.

The village of Kelmscott is on the Oxfordshire side of the
Thames, in wooded country, with broad meadows, 'all butter-
cuppy', as Morris put it, and stone houses with the stone-slated
roofs which endure for centuries and merely grow more
beautiful with age, and which are, as Morris said, 'the most
lovely covering which a roof can have'. There is a village stores,
a post-office, a small church, with the grave-yard in which
Morris is buried, a few scattered grey stone houses, and a pro-
found peace. Mackail declares, 'The country in which Kelmscott lies is among the sleepiest and loneliest of southern England.
With little bold or striking beauty, it has a charm of unequalled
subtlety and lastingness. The young Thames winds through
level pastures, among low surrounding hills, in a landscape that

seems as if little change had passed over it since the English settlement. Beyond the level and often flooded river-meadows the ground rises imperceptibly northwards towards the spurs of the Cotswolds, out of which half a dozen small rivers break to mingle with the Thames.' He adds that 'much of the domestic building of this region is little inferior to the churches either in age or architectural beauty'.

The Manor House lies at the end of the road which runs through the village, and a cart-track extends along one side of the high stone wall which encloses the garden. The gables of the house and the mullioned windows rise above the wall, a 'mass of grey walls and pearly grey roofs', Morris called it, and the beauty of this grey Tudor mass is quite astonishing.

We had already been told in the village that we could not go into the house as it was being restored after having been allowed to fall into a state of decay, but the Society of Antiquaries, of which Morris had been a member, had received a legacy and had donated £20,000 for the restoration of Kelmscott Manor. It had been in danger of becoming a ruin because it had been impossible to carry out the terms of Mary Morris's will regarding it. She had inherited it from her mother on her death, and on her own death in 1938 it went to Oxford University with an endowment of £3000; it had been her idea that it should provide a home for retired professors of Exeter, her father's college, and the Slade School of Arts, the Bodleian Library, and the Ashmolean Museum were similarly to make use of it, but the endowment was inadequate to administer the bequest. As no other funds were available the house was let to a succession of private tenants, until eventually the will clause was made invalid by the High Court and the property went to the residuary legatee, the Society of Antiquaries, who, until they received the legacy, were unable to do anything about it, so it ust stood there mouldering away, as untenanted, uncared-for houses do, with its lovely garden running wild, an ironic state of affairs, as Alan Wykes, who visited it just before the legacy was received, points out,[1] for the home of the principal founder of the Society for the Protection of Ancient Buildings. It should have been possible, one feels, to have found some good use for the beautiful old place once it had reverted to the Antiquaries.[2]

We drove on through the lovely unspoiled Oxfordshire countryside, with its lush meadows and its lanes bordered with cow-parsley, to the little riverside town of Lechlade, in Gloucestershire. A large church dominates the high street at one end, and there are old houses; the River Coln joins the Thames here, and it is a pleasant enough town, but of no special interest, and we continued on another mile or so to Fairford—the Fair Ford on the Coln, the Manor of Fairford, part of the 'Honour of Gloucestershire', a small beautiful grey stone town with a beautiful Tudor-Gothic church which is virtually a museum of mediaeval glass. The 'fair new church at Fairford', described by John Leland, the fifteenth-century antiquary in his famous *Itinerary*, was built at the end of that century by John Tame, a rich wool merchant, and finished by his second son, Sir Edmund. In his scholarly guide book to the church Mr. O. G. Farmer tells us that 'in the latter part of the fifteenth and the early part of the sixteenth century a wave of rebuilding set in throughout this part of the country, and such fine examples of the perpendicular style, as those existing at Northleach, Cirencester, Winchombe, and elsewhere, were being erected as monuments of the gratitude to Almighty God of the great woolmen and cloth workers for the wealth and prosperity which were theirs'.

I think this church, dedicated to St. Mary the Virgin, is the most beautiful I was ever in. Mr. Farmer says that the 'most inexperienced eye can see that no expense was spared to make this, the House of God, as beautiful as possible'; but it is not expense which it suggests but a very fine architectural taste. It is

1. In his book *An Eye on the Thames*, 1966.
2. Now restored, it has a tenant in residence.

all of the local stone, and the lofty arches, and the traceries of the windows, have been most delicately carved. The tower, at the centre of the church, is older, though of the same century; John Tame, when he received permission to demolish the old building and create his fair new church, retained the tower, as relatively modern, but made some alterations to it, making the arch leading to the nave wider, and giving the lantern a handsome groined vault. The view through the arches of the tower to the east window, which depicts the Passion, is completely wonderful.

The west window is devoted to the Last Judgment, with Christ at the centre come to judge the quick and the dead; he holds a lily in one hand and a sword in the other; his throne is a rainbow, and the earth is his footstool; behind and around him is a radiance of ruby red, in which angels are to be made out. The richness of the colouring of this mediaeval glass is beyond description. It was John Tame's intention to make the windows tell the gospel story. 'Stained-glass windows had been employed for didactic purposes from a much earlier date,' Oscar Farmer says in his guide, 'but necessarily with much more limited scope. But now the glazier's art had so far advanced as to admit of more extended schemes, and the broader windows lent themselves much better to continuous narrative than their lancet predecessors.' He calls them a 'great illuminated book', divided into three main chapters, with an introduction, and with chapter one beginning in the Lady Chapel. There would appear to be good evidence for believing that the glass was made by the Flemish school of glaziers of whom Barnard Flower was the chief. He was given the contract for the windows in King's College Chapel, Cambridge, but died when he had completed only four of them.

At the outbreak of the Second World War the Church Council were concerned for the safety of the windows, and Mr. Oscar Farmer suggested storing them in the stone vaults under the big house in Fairford Park. This was agreed upon, and Mr. Farmer did the job, single-handed, beginning with the east window. When peace came he was asked to replace the glass, and began the great task in September, 1945. Again he worked single-handed, and the work took him two years, because repairs were necessary to the stone before the glass could be refitted. Writing in 1955, in a supplementary note to the church guide, he reports, with justifiable pride, that 'the work was completed in July, 1947, without accident of breakage either in the taking out, or in the transport, or in the replacement'.

At Kempsford, a pleasant village of stone houses with stone-slated roofs, and the Thames narrow and swift-flowing, with swans, there was another church, the Church of Edward the Confessor, and another Norman nave, and some good modern and a little old glass. It was very peaceful there, with no sound but the cawing of rooks in the high elms, and we lingered a little before following the Thames to Cricklade in Wiltshire, and on to Kemble in Gloucestershire. We were then on the Cirencester road, and very close to Thames Head.

Cirencester is, I think, my second favourite place in England after Winchester. It has narrow streets, grey stone gabled houses, seventeenth century, built by the rich wool merchants, and a huge park behind an enormous yew hedge topping a high stone wall. For centuries Cirencester had importance as a wool town, as the town nearest the head of the river, and as a coaching stop; its decline came in the nineteenth century, with the advent of the railway, and the loss of its wool trade to Yorkshire. Now it is a tourist centre for the Cotswolds, and a hunting and agricultural centre, with factories for the production of agricultural implements. The grass grows among the sleepers of its disused railway station, but a considerable volume of traffic pours through its main street; its great days are over, but it is still a lively country town, and one of character.

But its great glory is its huge and splendid parish church of St. John the Baptist, which, in the words of the late Archdeacon J. S. Sinclair, a former Vicar of Cirencester, is 'larger than three cathedrals . . . and one of the most spacious churches in England'. It dates from Norman times but is mainly Perpendicular. The tower, supported by two large flying buttresses, was built in 1400; the enormous south porch in 1500. This porch is a building in itself, and despite its date has, like the old Guildhall at Norwich, a nineteenth-century look, and it was, in fact, rebuilt, stone for stone, in 1836; in 1908 more restoration had to be carried out, to the foundations and to the decaying external stonework; more work was done on it in 1954. After the Dissolution the upper chamber was used for a time as the Town Hall, and permission was granted in 1672 for it to be let for public purposes. The east window is beautiful with pale mediaeval glass, fifteenth century, and there is even older glass, thirteenth century, in the St. John's Chapel. The nave is beautiful with lofty pillars and arches, and there is an interesting and beautiful pulpit, dating from the fifteenth century, and the shape of a wine glass. It is of open stone tracery, and is one of the few pre-Reformation pulpits in the country.

If I do this beautiful and noble church less than justice it is because I came to it whilst still under the spell of Fairford. There have been a great many churches, large and small, in this book, to be sure, but you cannot take in the English scene without them; they are not only an important part of its landscape, but of the history of the towns and villages in which they stand. They form a national heritage of interest and beauty, for believer and unbeliever alike.

Thames Head, as I have said, is not easy to find, there being nothing to indicate the turning off the Cirencester road leading to the meadow which contains it; and when you get there the source may appear to have dried up; on the other hand the field may be watery, as on the day I was there, and difficult to negotiate.

But the infant river is always there, a narrow stream meandering between hawthorn trees, and that this is the genesis of the great river that flows past the Houses of Parliament, that becomes the Pool of London, and broadens out into the reaches of Gravesend and the estuary, seems incredible. In 1958 the Thames Conservancy put up a statue of a reclining Neptune-like figure, 'Father Thames', holding a wooden paddle and surrounded by bales and bundles representing commerce and trade, and a barrel which suggests beer—whether that was the sculptor's intention or not. The arms of the City of London are carved on a stone shield; there is a railing round the statue, and at the side of it a notice which says that it was placed there 'to mark the source of the River Thames', and that it was given by by H. Scott Freeman, Esq. The notice does not say so, but it was originally in the grounds of the Crystal Palace.

The initials, T.H., were at some time carved on the ash tree that leans out over the heap of stones guarding the spring, but the years have now almost obliterated them, and the statue, even if it is no great work of art, was a good idea.

The little stream at Thames Head has to flow for 209 miles before it reaches the sea at the Nore. By the time it reaches Oxford it is 150 feet wide; at London Bridge 250 feet, at Gravesend over 2000 feet, and between Sheerness and Shoeburyness, immediately above the Nore, five and a half miles.

Cirencester, although it is the nearest town to Thames Head, is not a Thames town, its river being the Churn, which joins the town at Lechlade. In his book, *An Eye on the Thames*, Alan Wykes tells a pleasant story of Elizabeth I arriving at Lechlade in the summer of 1592 and demanding to be borne in her litter along the river bank 'to the very first trickle of my fyne Thames', on her way to Cirencester, where her host, Sir John Danvers, presented her with 'a fayre cuppe of double gilt

wirth xx £, given by the town of Cyseter with an oration
made in Latyn'.

I was glad that my English journey, which began in the grey
days of March with London's river, at Greenwich and Gravesend, ended in the Mede in Gloucestershire in the warm butter-
cup days of June, at Thames Head. The book began with a
return to source; it is right that it should end with one.

Index